# FROM MONS TO MALI

FOR
RICHARD GLANFRWYDD THOMAS
WELCH REGIMENT
(attached SEAFORTH HIGHLANDERS AND SHERWOOD FORESTERS)
EGYPT, LIBYA, TUNISIA, SICILY AND ITALY
1941–1946

# FROM MONS TO MALI

## Fifty Extraordinary and Little-Known Vignettes of British and Commonwealth Airmen in Action Since 1914

## ANDREW THOMAS

GRUB STREET • LONDON

Published by
Grub Street
4 Rainham Close
London SW11 6SS

Copyright © Grub Street 2022
Copyright text © Andrew Thomas 2022

A CIP record for this title is available from the British library

ISBN-13: 978-1-911667-40-7

Design by Myriam Bell Design UK

Printed and bound by Finidr, Czech Republic

# CONTENTS

# PART 3: POST-WORLD WAR     141

# FOREWORD

Air Commodore Hamish Cormack CBE
Deputy Commandant, Defence Academy

Air Commodore Hamish Cormack CBE

This book is made up of a series of brief snapshots – actions and incidents some of which took place over breathless seconds or minutes that must have felt like hours. There is a golden thread that runs through the decades from the first story to the last; the human experience of operating and fighting in the air. The air is not our natural habitat. Gravity is defied, weather endured, the extremes of altitude overcome and all with the constant knowledge that, if things go wrong, the ground ultimately has a 'probability of kill' of one – in other words, high-speed impact with terra firma hurts. Then there are risks like mechanical malfunction, collision or misidentification resulting in 'blue-on-blue'. Add in the enemy and their concerted effort to make your day far worse, and what you have is an environment that is multi-dimensional, fast paced and unforgiving. Mastering or just enduring these challenges bonds all those who have shared the experience. My own operational duties have included counter-terrorism in Northern Ireland, counter-insurgency in Iraq, counter-narcotics in Afghanistan, the air campaigns in Libya and Syria, disaster-relief operations in Pakistan and military aid to the civilian authorities in the UK. On the scale of mastering to just enduring, my efforts fall closer to the latter description, but I can relate to those with far more prowess and heroism through the tales told in this book, and I am sure you will feel that connection too.

In these pages you may find the familiar but hopefully the new and surprising too – I know I did. Even readers with only a passing interest in aviation will immediately recognise British icons like the ubiquitous Spitfire and the unmistakable giant delta of the Vulcan. However, alongside these superstars are the less well-known supporting actors like the Vickers Wellesley, CAC Wirraway and Westland Wyvern too. The book spans time; from when taking to the air may have been as much a choice of what not to do, an escape from the realities of the trenches, to the vocational professional air forces of today. The technology has evolved at a remarkable pace, from canvas, dope and the 'Mark 1 eyeball', to supersonic platforms bristling with highly automated and integrated sensors. This book also takes the reader on a journey around the world; from the exotic to the remote – Eritrea and New Guinea to the Aleutians – but closer to home too – Tyneside and York. And while the environment of the air is the common theme, in many stories land and sea are inextricably linked too, bringing their own characters and challenges. So, this is a story of aviation, time, place and environment… but most of all, of people; the men and women who fly, maintain and support.

The tales contained are told from the perspective of British and Commonwealth aircrew. The link is not just one of past or present relation to the United Kingdom, it is also one of common values. However, in most tales there is an enemy too; a necessarily loaded phrase. It is worth pondering that those who were met in combat viewed 'us' as their enemy. While it may be said that time will judge who was on the 'right side of history', individual actions are liable to be motivated by much more personal or prosaic reasons – the desire to protect loved ones and ways of life, the fear of letting down those to your left and right, and that sense of camaraderie and loyalty to brothers and sisters-in-arms. But going back to the shared bond of those who operate in the air, then there is also a common language and experience that links friend and foe, potentially offering an avenue for reconciliation after the fighting has stopped. There are many instances of former adversaries in the air meeting after the conflicts have cooled, finding mutual respect and understanding. Dialogue is a constructive force and this sense of shared experience offers hope amidst tales of war and conflict.

The stories within have a very personal tone. It is not hard to imagine the narrowing of vision as a tiny dot on the horizon rapidly emerges into the form of a mortal threat. You can relate to the surge of adrenaline as the hands reach for the yellow and black handle that will fire the ejection seat from the cocoon of the cockpit into the unforgiving elements. The slight tightening of grip on the collective and cyclic levers can almost be felt, as the hover is held amidst the smoke and fire of the burning ship below. While such moments, single tactical events, may seem to have little impact on the course of a conflict and history, for the individual or crews involved at that time it was their all, with the ever-incumbent danger of failure and sacrifice. Without these individual actions, there is no operational and strategic effect, it really is the sum of the many parts and those parts are deeply individual in experience.

Starting and ending with a story from 5 Squadron, from Mons to Mali, the author emphasises the echoes of history. While the young airmen in Mons 1914 may have been incredulous if shown the Sentinel of the future, they would have immediately recognised the maple leaf of their squadron stitched onto the flying suits of their present-day compatriots. I also hope and believe they would have recognised the spirit, professionalism, humility and humour of the squadron, their squadron, on the Mali detachment of 2013 too. There is a wealth of tales beyond those captured here that will engage, excite and inspire, so I look forward with great anticipation to future volumes. The biggest challenge is choosing which ones to select and I do not envy Andrew that task!

This is a chronicle laced with the courage, fear, resilience, hope and despair of the moment, but also the enduring spirit of those involved resonating across time. I hope you get as much out of reading this as I did. Let yourself be transported into the cockpits and cabins where the action took place, evoking the smells, sounds, sights and feelings that those who were there experienced.

# INTRODUCTION

The genesis of this book probably came from one of the last visits I had with my late father. From 1941 to 1946 he had been an infantry soldier serving with the 8th Army in North Africa and Italy, being twice wounded. His had, I believe, been a hard war of which he spoke little. At the time of the visit I had only recently returned from one of my regular trips to Afghanistan and my younger son who was an army officer was at the time serving there on secondment to the Afghan National Army and so the conversation moved from there onto my father's own war service. He spoke movingly of one particular incident after which he remarked that grand histories were written by generals or eminent historians whereas 'his' war was limited to what was 50 yards or so either side of him in a trench. Similar comments had been made several times by RAF veterans that I had interviewed, often saying that their perception of an action would be subtly different from someone in another aircraft, even if in the same formation. From my own experience on operations I would concur with both these reflections. Thus any campaign is composed of a myriad of small individual parts or, in the modern idiom of the computer screen picture, it is made up of an infinite number of pixels.

In addition to contributing as part of a team producing a detailed history of the Mediterranean Air War I have been working on a long-term project on RAF and Commonwealth air force battle honours. For this project I had assembled a considerable amount of material and images, some of which are precisely dated and relate to a specific incident. To occupy some time during the various covid lockdowns I explored the background to a number of the pictures that revealed some fascinating stories. Subsequently during one of the first events allowed after lockdown restrictions were lifted, I met John Davies of Grub Street, and publisher of the *A History of the Mediterranean Air War* series, and in between talk of cricket mentioned what I had been doing. He picked up on the idea and suggested that I produce a compilation for publication as a book. The idea of writing a series of interesting short narratives seemed appealing and I agreed to the proposal.

When the British Expeditionary Force went to war in August 1914 the small Royal Flying Corps accompanied it whilst the embryonic Royal Naval Air Service supported the Royal Navy; within days British airmen were in action. Since then men (and more recently women) flying in their successor services – the Royal Air Force, Fleet Air Arm and Army Air Corps – together with their sister services in the Commonwealth have been on near continuous operations.

This book presents a selection of 50 short stories covering campaigns from that first engagement at Mons to the present day. By a fortunate piece of serendipity one of the RAF's current operations is in Mali thus offering a very neat and alliterative title. I have deliberately included in this selection a significant number of accounts highlighting the contribution of the various Commonwealth air forces, whose histories have been so closely entwined with the RAF and which would be impossible to disentangle. It also provides the opportunity to explore many lesser-known campaigns and operations both from the world wars and elsewhere. I have also attempted to illustrate the full spread of roles and tasks that airmen have undertaken down the years.

Throughout the book I have used an image or a related artefact of a specific date or incident as the 'hook' for each chapter. Thus, whilst some of the individuals or actions described may be familiar to the reader, most will not. This is deliberate so as to feature both the heroic and the mundane that mix into the cornucopia of history more of which will feature, it is hoped, in a future volume – *Flanders to the Falklands*.

There is a common thread among the individuals mentioned on the pages within this book. From the very first, the airmen of the British and Commonwealth air services have been volunteers; no one has ever been compelled to fly. These volunteers have also been selected and undergone lengthy training and from the very beginning to the present day, aircrew have been regarded as something of an elite. Some found fame and won many awards, but most did not. This is, I hope, a book about the many, not the few. There is also another common thread that links all the men and women who have flown on operations from Mons to Mali and everywhere in between. They did their duty.

Andrew Thomas
Heckington
March 2022

# ACKNOWLEDGEMENTS

In a book covering the breadth of air operations such as this I have drawn on a network of friends, researchers and official bodies who have all contributed information, from the smallest, but essential, snippet to the fruits of their own researches. To each I offer my thanks and appreciation for their assistance and forbearance in fielding sometimes obscure and seemingly inconsequential queries. To list every individual would take a book in itself, but most are named within the credits in individual chapters or the bibliography.

From some there has been broader support that I should wish to acknowledge. I am especially grateful to my friend and former colleague Air Commodore Hamish Cormack for contributing such an eloquent and thoughtful foreword, particularly given the time constraints of his current post. Vic Flintham, Chris Shores, Chris Thomas and Air Commodore Graham Pitchfork, all long-standing friends, have been particularly supportive in offering both practical help and sound advice on the project; their books as well as the archive material given to me by the late Peter Green were never far from hand. Others too have always given me the benefit of their particular researches with the unparalleled knowledge of Martin Goodman on Hurricanes and of Peter Arnold and Wojtek Matusiak on Spitfires being often tapped. Good friends Colin Huston, Mick Davis, Andy Kemp and Trevor Henshaw of the Cross and Cockade Society of WW1 air historians provided invaluable information. So too Wg Cdr Jeff Jefford (one of my instructors all those years ago!) who's delving into the minutiae of RAF organisation is always so valued by researchers. Help from colleagues and fellow enthusiasts overseas too has been inestimable. In Australia Russell Guest is a mine of material while in Italy Giovanni Massimello has regularly provided information of opponents in combats, as did Theo Boiten for Luftwaffe night fighters. From South Africa generous support came from Lionel Reid (who has selflessly shared material from his own forthcoming book), Steven MacLean and from Stefaan Bouwer whilst the doyen of Canadian aviation publishing, Larry Milberry has always been ready with detailed and valuable responses. No aspect of the history of the Indian Air Force could be covered without the generous assistance of Air Marshal Vikram Singh whilst the inputs from P. V. S. Jagan Mohan, editor of the wonderfully detailed Bahrat Rakshak website, too were invaluable.

No history research would be possible without the helpful co-operation of official bodies and in the UK the Air Historical Branch headed by Sebastian Cox have been ever helpful, with Mike Hatch and Neil Chamberlain deserving special thanks. I am specially grateful to Ms Andrea Sevier, head librarian of the RAF College, Cranwell, for access to that wonderful library. The staff of the excellent RAAF Museum at Point Cook, Victoria were so helpful whilst at the equally splendid Air Force Museum of New Zealand Matthew Wright combines knowledge of the RNZAF with great enthusiasm and deserves particular praise. So to for Mrs Janet Lacroix at the Digital Media Management Section at NDHQ Ottawa who is generous with both her time and expertise in answering queries and providing relevant imagery. Finally, I must thank the team at Grub Street for their expertise and advice, particularly to John Davies for suggesting and adopting the project, and to Natalie Parker for her editing skills and fine eye for detail.

To all, my sincere thanks and my hopes that the end result does not disappoint.

## PART 1

# WORLD WAR I AND THE INTERWAR YEARS

# THE FIRST OF MANY
## 22 August 1914

When war against Germany was declared on 4 August, 1914 the British Expeditionary Force (BEF) began moving to France. With it went most of the aircraft of the then new Royal Flying Corps for reconnaissance duties. Based at Gosport under Maj 'Jack' Higgins was 5 Squadron that was relatively well equipped with A and B Flights respectively under Capts D. G. Connor and R. Grey having eight Henri Farman F.20s whilst Capt George Carmichael's C Flight had four Avro 504s, a more modern design. Nos. 2, 3, 4 and 5 Squadrons were assigned to the BEF and immediately began mobilising. This included supplementing the service mechanical transport (MT) with requisitioned civilian vehicles, one of which was a red van advertising HP Sauce that was used to carry bombs and ammunition. It later became a useful marker to tired pilots trying to find the latest landing field during the retreat. Each flight was self-contained, including mobile workshop and stores vehicles. On 13 August, the CO and ground party sailed from Southampton and the next day the aircraft left Gosport for Dover, though several pilots had minor incidents. Capt Carmichael had to replace his Avro with a BE8 but the remainder then crossed safely to France and assembled at

Avro 504 No. 398, of 5 Squadron at Farnborough on 29 July 1914 shortly before setting out for France. (RAE)

Avro 504s of 5 Squadron like 638 roamed north of Mons to establish the position of the Germans, though one was shot down on 22 August. (J. M. Bruce/G. S. Leslie Collection)

Amiens. The CO arrived there with the MT on the 16th while Carmichael was sent to Buc to select three new Henri Farmans to replace the damaged aircraft. The RFC then moved forward to Maubeuge alongside the HQ of the BEF where 5 Squadron arrived on the 18th. The move was marred when BE8 391 crashed badly injuring Lt Robert Smith-Barry but his passenger Cpl 'Ginger' Geard was killed.

By 19 August 5 Squadron had fully assembled with some new aircraft having been delivered, including another of the unpopular BE8s. The RFC flew its first reconnaissance sorties to the south of Brussels during the day but failed to locate either the enemy or the Belgian army. As the summer mist cleared the next day the RFC sorties returned with the disturbing news of the sighting of a vast German force advancing south of Brussels. Early on 21 August 5 Squadron flew its first war sortie when Lt Christopher Wilson with Lt Euan Rabagliati as observer flew a reconnaissance ahead of the advancing BEF as it moved into southern Belgium. At Namur, Wilson and Rabagliati discovered the massed German cavalry of Gen Georg von der Marwitz's Cavalry Corps that were reconnoitring ahead of Gen Alexander von Kluck's First Army as it swept on its wide enveloping movement. This was important news and on return was duly reported to GHQ. At dawn the following morning, Saturday 22 August, north of Mons near Maisières C Squadron of the 4th Royal Irish Dragoon Guards under Major Tom Bridges had the first, brief, skirmish with the German army.

The RFC sent out reconnaissance sorties though the day that revealed further confirmation of the massive German enveloping movement. Among them was 5 Squadron Avro 504 '390' flown by Lts Vincent Waterfall and Gordon Bayly that left Maubeuge just after 1015hrs. They flew about 15 miles north of Mons and at 1050hrs on the Mons-Soignies road they noted around 600 baggage wagons making for Thieusies. Twenty

minutes later near Enghien they descended to about 2,000ft after spotting about 600 cavalry in file and four companies of infantry as well as six four-horse gun teams noting the column turning towards Silly.

It was the last entry in their report as the aircraft was engaged by intense rifle fire from a

**Left and right respectively:** Lt Vincent Waterfall and Lt Gordon Bayly became the first British airmen to be killed in action when shot down on 22 August. (CCI)

company of the advancing 12th Brandenburg Grenadiers led by Hptm Walter Bloem, a famous novelist, who recalled the incident: "I ordered the two groups to fire at it... the plane started a half-turn, but it was too late; it went into a dive, spun around several times then fell like a stone about a mile from here."

The aircraft was hit and crashed, killing both men instantly; Waterfall and Bayly were the first British airmen to be killed in action. Their RFC uniforms also provided the Germans the first information of the presence of the British ahead of them. The

Germans buried them in a shallow grave, saluted and moved on. Later, Belgian civilians reburied the bodies of the airmen and they also found Bayly's torn and charred report. This was later sent to the British HQ, its last entry reading: "11.00hrs, cavalry, 4 columns infantry, other group of horses and column turning left to Silly."

Lt Bayly's partially completed report that was recovered by Belgian civilians and passed to the GHQ of the British Expeditionary Force. (British Official)

# THE RFC'S FIRST BOMBING ATTACK
# 10 March 1915

Capt Louis Strange received the MC for his exploits during the Battle of Neuve Chapelle, particularly for mounting the first bombing attack by the RFC.
(6 Squadron Records)

At the start of 1915 the British lines in France stretched continuously through Flanders from Langemarck in the Ypres Salient as to join the French along the La Bassée Canal at Givenchy. After a very trying winter in the muddy trenches of the Lys valley it was decided to open an offensive as soon as conditions allowed. By early March with the ground beginning to dry plans for an attack were made aimed at the capture of the village of Neuve Chapelle and then to establish lines as far forward as possible to the east. The initial attack was to be by 40,000 men of the IVth Corps and the Indian Corps along a two-mile front before which the RFC squadrons conducted the systematic photographing of the German trench system to a depth of 1,500 yards around Neuve Chapelle.

Ahead of the offensive, on 8 March the 11 BE2s of 6 Squadron based at Bailleul under Maj Gordon Shephard as part of the RFC's Second Wing moved north to Poperinghe leaving a detachment of wireless-equipped aircraft at Bailleul. One of the squadron's flight commanders was Capt Louis Strange, who was among the most forward-thinking pilots in the RFC.

In dull, misty conditions, shortly before 0700hrs on 10 March a concentrated artillery bombardment along a 2,000-yard line by 342 guns opened the attack at Neuve Chapelle. The fire was partly directed by aircraft and initially the infantry was very successful such that by midday the village had been captured. However, strengthening resistance and conflicting information meant that the initial success could not be

Flying BE 2c 1748 on 10 March Capt Louis Strange mounted a successful bombing attack on Courtrai railway station. (E. Ferko)

immediately exploited. Through the day flights in direct support were attempted and met with variable success but were for the most part unsuccessful, largely due to the poor visibility created by the mist and smoke from the battle. However, ahead of the assault, plans had previously been made by the RFC for attacks on railway targets likely to be important for the movement of enemy reinforcements to the battle area.

As well as attempting to directly support the assault during the day, 6 Squadron also mounted a very notable operation. At 1523hrs Louis Strange took off from Poperinghe in BE2c 1748 which he had modified to carry four 20lb bombs on rudimentary wing racks of his own design which could be released by pulling a cable from the cockpit. He also carried some hand grenades in the cockpit. Strange headed for Courtrai and the railway station through which reinforcements were reported passing heading to Neuve Chapelle. He was followed at 1530hrs by Capt George Carmichael of 5 Squadron in a Martinsyde S.1 who headed for Menin.

Flying below the cloud base at 3,000 feet in poor visibility after almost becoming lost in the misty conditions, when crossing the lines Strange encountered some anti-aircraft fire. Despite the testing conditions, on arriving over Courtrai he spotted the railway station. On descending to 150ft he was fired at by a sentry on the platform so he promptly responded and dropped a hand grenade on him. In the face of a heavy barrage

Ground crew prepare BE2c 1756 for another sortie from Poperinghe at the time of the battle in March 1915. (C. Huston)

of rifle fire from troops on the platforms he also observed two trains standing at the station. Strange then positioned the BE2 and ran in releasing his bombs on the trains as he flew overhead. The explosions left 75 dead and many injured resulting in the station remaining closed for three days. On his return to Poperinghe a dozen bullet hits were found on the aircraft. The attack was later favourably referred to by the commander of the BEF, Field Marshal Sir John French, and was regarded as the first pre-planned and executed bombing mission by the RFC.

Two weeks later Strange was awarded the MC:

"For gallantry and ability on reconnaissance and other duties on numerous occasions, especially on the occasion when he dropped three bombs from a height of only 200 feet on the railway junction at Courtrai, whilst being assailed by heavy rifle fire."

# FORM SQUARE!
# 11 May 1916

In a throwback to late 19th century colonial campaigning against the Dervishes led by the Mahdi and the Khalifa, for some time operations had been in progress against Ali Dinar Zakariya Mohammed al-Fadl, the self-proclaimed Sultan of Darfur. It was estimated the Dervish Fur army comprised 800 regular cavalry, 3,000 regular infantry with rifles and perhaps up to 2,000 irregular spearmen all of which wore jibbahs and carried Islamic banners similar to those worn at Omdurman in 1898. It was decided to send a detachment of aircraft to the Sudan to support these operations so on 20 April 1916 C Flight, 17 Squadron under Capt Edgar Bannatyne was ordered to move to the Sudan. Two airstrips at Nahud, 270 miles south-west of Khartoum and an advanced strip at Jebel el Hilla were hurriedly prepared. All the logistics and spares to support the four BE2s had to be shipped by rail and river and thence overland by truck and camel. It therefore took almost three weeks to get C Flight to a position at Jebel el Hilla to support the column as it was now the hottest time of the year when violent *haboobs* or dust storms were frequent, making flying hazardous.

BE2c 4455 of C Flight lands at Rahad after a test flight on 5 May 1916 before heading to support the Field Force in Darfur. (Sir John Slessor via J. M. Bruce)

Ali Dinar's capital at El Fasher was 180 miles to the north-west across the desert from the strip at Nahud. The first two BE2s, 5554 flown by Lt F. Bellamy and 2/Lt John Slessor in 4455 landed at Jebel el Hilla after dawn on 11 May where Capt Bannatyne and some mechanics had set up canvas

**Above left:** During Darfur operations C Flight was led by Capt Edgar Bannatyne who later received the DSO. (J. M. Bruce/G. S. Leslie Collection)

**Above right:** Lt F. Bellamy was one of the three pilots who moved to the forward base during the Darfur operation. (J. M. Bruce/G. S. Leslie Collection)

hangars and stores. The other two aircraft would remain in reserve at Nahud. A forward point had also been established at the Abiad Wells. The following morning Lt Bellamy flew the first reconnaissance to El Fasher where he dropped the Sirdar's proclamation urging the population to move away but to which the sultan sent an insolent letter in response. Bellamy also landed near the Field Force to make a personal report to the commander, Lt Col Kelly. The decisive action began with the Field Force forming a square formation of infantry with transport, artillery and stores in the centre to repel cavalry attack. Marching across the desert, the 'square' moved at about 20 miles per day. The aircraft reconnoitred ahead keeping villages under observation, dropping messages to the square by bags attached to coloured streamers. On the 17th Capt Bannatyne was flying low over Meleit where he spotted about 500 Dervishes and having been heavily fired on attacked them with bombs and machine-gun fire before they dispersed. During two sorties that day he spent nine hours in the air. During a five-hour sortie the next morning 2/Lt John Slessor in 4459 covered the 'square' when it arrived at Meleit water hole, dropping a message to confirm the area was clear.

The column halted for a three-day rest during which the aircraft continued flying reconnaissance of El Fasher where the main Dervish force was located north of the town at Beringia. However, the weather then broke and thick dust and haze prevented flying, though both Bannatyne and Bellamy flew on the 22nd but were unable to see anything. The Field Force, still in its square, had moved towards El Fasher at dawn that day where

just to the north of the town the Dervishes attacked with fanatical courage, but wilted under modern gunfire. Predictably the battle resulted in the total defeat of the sultan's army and the column moved on and occupied the town.

2/Lt Slessor in 4554 about to leave Rahad for Jebel el Hilla on 11 May 1916 and later flew it to attack a force of Dervish cavalry with bombs and machine-gun fire. (J. M. Bruce/G. S. Leslie Collection)

At 0515hrs that morning 2/Lt John Slessor flying 4554 left Jebel el Hilla and after refuelling at an advanced strip laid out near the main force at Abiad Wells he flew towards El Fasher to cover the troops that were to enter the town. Spotting a force of around 2,000 Dervish cavalry Slessor attacked with bombs and machine-gun fire to great effect, causing utter terror and confusion and narrowly missing killing the sultan. This had a decisive effect and the morale of the enemy was broken by this unexpected attack. However, on Slessor's final pass to drop his last bomb the aircraft came under heavy fire and he was badly wounded in the thigh, flying back to Abiad moving the rudder control wire with his hand. He noted in his flying logbook: "…saw artillery fire and Dervish cavalry flying banners. Dropped bomb and fired mg. Came in about 2000 over S of town and bombed them with effect. Got shot in leg."

In his later dispatches the Sirdar (commander of the Anglo-Egyptian Army) was unstinting in his praise for the excellent work done in reconnaissance and bombing by the men of C Flight. Edgar Bannatyne later received the DSO for his part in the Darfur campaign. Sultan Ali Dinar escaped from Beringia but was killed by a Camel Corps patrol a few months later.

The Darfur capital at El Fasher seen from a C Flight BE2c. (USNA)

# ZEPPELIN KILLER
# 27 November 1916

To increase the defences against raids by Zeppelin airships on east coast towns, on 1 February 1916 36 Squadron was formed at Cramlington, Northumberland, under temporary command of Capt R. O. Abercrombie. Equipped with the BE2c it was responsible for the aerial defence of Newcastle, the Tees and Forth areas. For this B Flight was detached to Turnhouse near Edinburgh and C Flight to Seaton Carew just south of Hartlepool leaving A Flight at Cramlington. The squadron flew its first war sorties on the night of 1/2 April during a raid on northern England with two more flown against a further raid the following night. After a patrol against another Zeppelin raid on the night of 5 April, Capt John Nichol was killed when he crashed on landing in BE2c 2739 becoming 36 Squadron's first casualty. There was then little activity through the short summer nights, though during this period the development of incendiary ammunition significantly improved the effectiveness of the Home Defence squadrons against the Zeppelins.

At 1215hrs on 27 November Zeppelin L 21 lifted off from Nordholz in northern Germany beginning a major raid on north-east England. Twenty-five minutes later L 34 departed Nordholz. It was part of two groups of airships that split over the North Sea with four of them, L 24, L 34, L 35 and L 36 making for Tyneside. The latter three

Seen at Seaton Carew, BE2c 2738 of 36 Squadron was flown by Lt Ian Pyott to destroy Zeppelin L 34. (M. Davis)

Twenty-year-old Lt I. V. Pyott, of 36 Squadron was awarded the DSO for the destruction of the L 34. (M. Davis)

were new 485ft-long R-Class Super-Zeppelins. As the airships approached 36 Squadron was placed onto full alert and following a spurious report of five of them over Seaham harbour, 20-year-old South African Lt Ian Pyott took off from Seaton Carew on an uneventful patrol landing back at 2210hrs. At about that time Zeppelin L 34 under the experienced KpLt Max Dietrich crossed the coast at 9,000ft near Blackhall, Co Durham. After flying inland, the huge airship turned south and was caught by searchlights just west of Hartlepool where it dropped 13 bombs on Elwick before moving east, dropping further bombs on West Hartlepool. Dietrich then headed L 34 towards the coast where it was again illuminated by searchlights enabling anti-aircraft guns to open fire. Twenty-nine more bombs were dropped on the centre of the town that caused a significant number of casualties. The raid created an equal measure of fear, excitement and anger in Hartlepool.

In response, at 2211hrs 2/Lt Francis Turner took off from Seaton Carew in BE2c 7344 followed ten minutes later by Ian Pyott flying BE2c 2738. After patrolling in the pitch black for just over an hour, at 2330hrs Lt Pyott spotted the L 34 that was held by the searchlight at Castle Eden. It was heading towards him and he dived his BE2 towards it as he described afterwards:

"I was at 9,800 feet and the Zepp seemed a few hundred feet below me. I flew towards it and flew at right angles to and underneath him, amidships, firing as I went under."

When the airship turned sharply eastwards Pyott followed flying alongside and over the next five miles he intermittently fired almost a full drum of incendiaries from his Lewis gun, aiming at one spot on the port quarter, seeing his fire enter the airship's envelope. He continued:

"I was aiming at his port quarter and noticed first a small patch become incandescent where I had seen tracers entering his envelope. I first took it for a machine gun firing at me, but this patch rapidly spread and the next thing the whole Zepp was in flames"

KpLt Max Dietrich was the commander of L 34 on its ill-fated final flight. He was the uncle of the actress Marlene Dietrich. (M. Davis)

Within moments the huge Zeppelin was completely engulfed with flames and Pyott was close enough for his face to be scorched. L 34 eventually exploded. As it fell nose first it broke into two with the larger section burning fiercely and crashing into Tees Bay half a mile off the Headland shore with the loss of Dietrich and his crew of 20. 2/Lt Turner was also in the area and had been about to attack L 34 when it caught fire and he spotted Pyott's aircraft in the glare.

The gruesome inferno was witnessed by KpLt Heinrich Hollander of the Zeppelin L 22: "There appeared a crimson ball of fire, which rapidly increased in size. A minute later we recognised the glowing skeleton of an airship falling in flames."

The L 34 was still burning when Ian Pyott landed back at Seaton Carew though he was half frozen as his colleagues lifted him from the cockpit cheering and chaired him away on their shoulders. Subsequently, he awarded the DSO.

An artist impression of the blazing L 34 over Hartlepool on 27 November 1916 from a contemporary newspaper. (M. Davis)

# SCHOOLBOY PILOT
## 25 January 1918

2/Lt Reginald Pohlmann RFC shortly after joining 25 Squadron just after his 19th birthday. (Author's Collection)

It has oft been stated that the life expectancy of a new Royal Flying Corps pilot in France during WW1 was around three weeks, the genre being of barely trained young men, straight out of school. While the figure may be allegorical, the fact is that life on a squadron in France was measured in weeks rather than months. One such teenage 'schoolboy' pilot 2/Lt Reginald Peel Pohlmann from Hipperholme near Halifax in the West Riding of Yorkshire was born on 4 August 1898.

Having volunteered in 1916, Reggie Pohlmann was called for service in February 1917 with the RFC, joining 41 Training Squadron (TS) at Doncaster. His first dual instruction sortie was on 10 June by Capt Chester Duffus lasting 40 minutes in Shorthorn 7059 with three landings. He then received further training at 11 TS at Spittalgate including experience on 'operational' types such as the BE2e and FK8 before going to 51 TS at Waddington for operational training on the DH4. After a final test on 1 September 2/Lt Reggie Pohlmann was passed out as a trained day bomber pilot – with a total of 52 hours 10 minutes flying time despite having never done any aerial gunnery nor dropped a bomb in practice.

On 25 September, Reggie Pohlmann joined 25 Squadron at Auchel north-west of Arras flying the DH4 and which was commanded by Maj Chester Duffus, his first instructor. He had joined as the bloody Third Battle of Ypres continued to the north. His first sortie with 25 Squadron was a test flight in DH4 A7487 two days later that was followed by several familiarisation flights over the Armentières–Arras sector with

With 51 TS at Waddington Reggie Pohlmann flew Martinsyde G.102 Elephant A4002 on 21, 22 and 27 August 1917. (J. M. Bruce/G. S. Leslie Collection)

Lt Bliss as observer. Finally, on 2 October, again with Bliss, Pohlmann flew his first combat sortie when in A7602 he dropped eight 20lb Cooper bombs from 16,500ft on gun emplacements near Cowrières. These were followed by further patrols and on 11 October the squadron moved north to Boisdinghem near St Omer. Pohlmann flew a bombing sortie with Lt Walsh in A7672 the next day. Bombing attacks continued for the rest of the month with Reggie Pohlmann flying seven, including a long-range attack on Ghent on the 20th when two 112lb bombs were dropped. On the 31st he dropped a 230 pounder on a train at Roulers behind the Ypres line.

On 23 November to support the offensive as Cambrai he dropped two 112lb bombs on Denain station with 2/AM C. N. Harvey in A7697 but his next successful operation was not until 2 December when with Lt Creek in A7609 he took part in

On the afternoon of 31 August 1917 Reggie Pohlmann flew his first solo in the de Havilland DH4 in A7546. (RAF Waddington)

a bombing raid. This was followed by a recce of the Lys Valley the next day when Lt Creek exposed 16 photo-plates. Following some leave Reggie flew a long-range recce south of Bruges on 28 December bringing back 17 photos. 2/Lt Pohlmann's first sortie of 1918 was an eventful three-hour reconnaissance in DH4 A7535 on 4 January when 36 plates were taken. He wrote afterwards:

> "While returning from a photographic reconnaissance, we were attacked by seven [Albatros] scouts [south of Cambrai]. We charged right through them at 130 mph. One enemy aircraft did a stall turn under our fuselage at about 50 yards range. The observer, 2/Lt O. S. Hinson, fired about 80 rounds and the machine was seen to turn on its back and dive down apparently out of control. The remainder could not keep up with us but followed firing at us from long range."

Poor weather precluded much flying but to establish the extent of the German build-up in the west following the collapse of Russia the previous year reconnaissance was the order of the day. Thus at 1145hrs on 25 January in DH4 A7865, with Lt Creek, Pohlmann flew a long reconnaissance to the fortress town of Mauberge and the rail centre at Valenciennes, the crew taking 32 photos. After this flight Reggie Pohlmann recorded his total flying time as 76 hours 10 minutes. It was the final entry in his logbook.

His next sortie was a bombing raid into Belgium on 5 February when he flew DH4 A7865 with 2/AM Roy Ireland as gunner. Leaving Boisdinghem soon after lunch the formation crossed the lines but one and a half hours later at 1440hrs it was attacked by the blue-nosed Albatros scouts of Jasta 36 led by Ltn Heinrich Bongartz. Shortly afterwards Bongartz attacked Pohlmann's DH4 which fell in flames near Oudenburg killing both the crew.

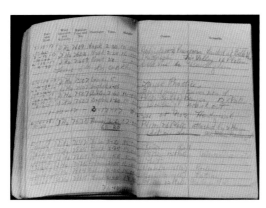

Reggie Pohlmann's logbook showing the final entry on 25 January 1918. (Author's Collection)

2/Lt Reginald Peel Pohlmann was buried just north of Pittem but after the war was re-interred at the Harlebeke New British Cemetery near Courtrai. He was 19½ years old.

# THE GREATEST AIR BATTLE
# 4 June 1918

When in February 1917 the Germans resumed unrestricted submarine warfare, U-boats of the Flandern (Flanders) Flotilla based in Belgium were soon taking a huge toll on British shipping. Air patrols over the North Sea were seen as one way to counter them by hampering their transits to and from their bases. A North Sea patrol matrix, later named 'the Spider Web', with the North Hinder light vessel as its datum was therefore developed. These patrols were flown by large Felixstowe and Curtiss flying boats of the Royal Naval Air Service based at Yarmouth and Felixstowe and where at the latter they were formed into the War Flight. To counter them, from September Hansa-Brandenburg W.12 and later W.29 floatplanes based at the Seeflugstations at Zeebrugge in Flanders and Borkum in the Frisian Islands went onto the offensive presaging regular fights with the RNAS flying boats. However, despite its size the 5½-ton Felixstowe F2A flying boat was no slouch when it came to aerial fighting.

There were regular encounters over the North Sea but the most memorable was on 4 June 1918 when three boats from the War Flight, Felixstowe F2As N4302 flown by Capt Barker, Lt Galvayne and Ens Kep USN and N4533 crewed by Capt Robert Dickey, Capt Paul, Lt Hodgson along with Lts Duff-Fyfe and Pattison and Ens Eaton

USN in Curtiss H-12 8689 with two more F2As (N4295 and N4298) from Yarmouth led by Capt Robert Leckie set out to avenge the loss on 30 May of Yarmouth-based H-12 8660 with

Felixstowe F2A N4533 with a Hansa-Brandenburg seaplane overhead strafing during the epic fight on 4 June 1918. (via J. Guttman)

After being strafed by a W.29 seaplane flown by Ltn z See Freidrich Christiansen Felixstowe F2A N4533 was left in flames on the water. (CCI)

Capt Young's crew. However, having crossed the North Sea near the Haaks Light Vessel ten miles from Terschelling in the Frisian Islands N4533 suffered an engine failure and alighted on the water. Dickey signalled that he had a broken petrol feed pipe and the boat would be unable to take off. As it was taxied towards Terschelling with the remaining four British boats circling protectively above, the crippled Felixstowe was attacked by five seaplanes that appeared from the base at Borkum. These intruders were driven off and were pursued by Lt Duff-Fyfe in the H-12 but this was then attacked and shot down by Germans and also force-landed in the North Sea off the northern tip of Vlieland.

Soon afterwards at 1630hrs German reinforcements in the form of ten more seaplanes appeared so Capt Robert Leckie put the remaining British aircraft into a 'vee' formation and went head on into the attackers exchanging fire in broadsides. This was repeated as they passed a second time, now in line astern. However, two of the F2As also had problems with their fuel pipes and had to effect makeshift repairs while in the middle of the action. Despite this the three flying boats continued to engage the German seaplanes meeting them in this remarkable air combat. One large enemy seaplane was forced down and landed heavily on the sea, a second was shot down before the remainder headed back but not before another had been forced down to make repairs and three more badly damaged. However, during the battle Lt Vernon Galvayne the observer in N4302 was killed by German fire. After the greatest air battle over the North Sea Robert Leckie led his small force back to Yarmouth. In his report he bitterly remarked: "...these operations were robbed of complete success entirely through faulty petrol pipes. It is obvious that our greatest foes are not the enemy..."

Having continued on the surface towards the Dutch coast N4533 was set on fire when attacked 200 yards off shore by Oblt z See Christiansen in Brandenburg W.29 No. 2239. Capt R. F. L. Dickey, Capt R. J. Paul, Lt A. G. Hodgson, 2/AM E. P. C. Bunton and AC H. Russell made it ashore where they were interned. The crew of the H-12 8689 were picked up by a Dutch trawler and Lt M. J. R. Duff-Fyfe, Lt J. R. Pattison, Ens J. A. Eaton USN, 1/AM E. J. Strewthers and Sgt A. J. Brown were also interned in the Netherlands. Despite the losses, after the battle Ltn z See Fritz Stormer who flew in the Staffel wrote: "Opposing enemy seaplane units in our area was comparatively easy to do, as our Hansa-Brandenburg monoplanes were superior to the British flying boats. Generally, the Staffel flew in a wedge formation with the Staffelkapitän in the leading seaplane."

One result of this action was that all the large flying boats had their hulls brightly painted in 'dazzle' patterns as Sqn Ldr Charles Snowdon-Gamble noted: "Pilots were allowed to paint their machines as they desired, and as a result the bizarre was not lacking." The schemes were charted and copies were held by units along the east coast for recognition. He also said that "…it was hoped that it would put the wind up the Hun".

Left: Oblt z See Friedrich Christiansen who destroyed N4533. (via J. Guttman)
Right: Capt Robert Leckie led the three surviving flying boats in the ferocious air battle with the German seaplanes. (via L. Milberry)

# 100 DAYS
# 25 August 1918

On 8 August 1918 the British opened a great offensive on the Somme at Amiens that was the first of a series of Allied offensives that were to end the war in a hundred days. One of the RAF units providing intimate support was 35 Squadron under Maj Kenneth Balmain flying the Armstrong Whitworth FK8 from Flesselles, just north of Amiens; it was part of 15 (Corps) Wing. After the success at Amiens, the next phase that was the final stage of the Battle of the Somme in 1918 was the battle for Bapaume, itself a preliminary to a wider assault. Prepared in secrecy, the assault on Bapaume began on 21 August and the initial attacks were covered by mist and low cloud that precluded any air support until mid-morning, six hours after the advance began.

No. 35 Squadron worked on the right flank of III Corps, bombing and strafing with some effect as well as conducting the more usual photographic and contact patrol work.

Typical was the three-hour-long sortie flown during the afternoon by 2/Lts Charles Strudwick and Adrian Weller. They took reconnaissance photographs just south of Albert near Méaulte when Weller fired 600 rounds into enemy-held trenches and though they spotted some German aircraft above, they were unmolested. The following day Albert was recaptured after very heavy fighting during which 35 Squadron FK8 C8644 flown by Lt Gerald Gunyon and 2/Lt Ernest Richardson was hit by machine-gun fire and force-landed near the town with a damaged radiator.

At dawn on 23 August the Battle of

Bapaume began in earnest on a front of 33 miles between Lihons and Arras as it was becoming evident that the German front was starting to unravel. Despite early mist 35 Squadron's patrols were out early with Strudwick and Weller supporting some tanks moving up south-east of Albert, though they had to force land due to the thickening fog. They later returned and flew another sortie later in the day. Progress was steady and the following day so rapid was the advance that some troops outstripped their supply lines and so 35 Squadron was regularly tasked with dropping supplies of ammunition from low level, often with astonishing accuracy. During one such sortie in the late afternoon FK8 D5154 was hit by machine-gun fire forcing Lt Malcolm Stewart and 2/Lt Herbert Howard to crash land across a trench, though they were uninjured.

During the evening 2/Lts Strudwick and Weller flew a lengthy contact patrol just north of the Somme between Mametz and Maricourt. They established that there were several German batteries east of the latter and attacked a party of enemy troops near Carnoy. The reconnaissance work kept the squadron's photographic section busy with over 3,000 prints a day often being produced. For the squadron's work through the day the commander of III Corps sent a congratulatory message praising "…the excellent work during the recent operations that has been of the greatest value".

Several contact patrols took off early on 25 August though some returned because of the thick mist, among them Lt Guy Haigh who noted in his logbook: "dud, ground mist. Returned." However, as visibility improved further sorties were successful and in mid-morning Haigh flying with 2/Lt Frank Powell spotted British cavalry advancing at a trot. Lt Melville Sonnenburg and 2/Lt John Clarke

The wreckage of Armstrong Whitworth FK8 F7374 which was shot down by German scouts when flown by Lts Strudwick and Weller on 25 August. (J. Michie via P. Holloway)

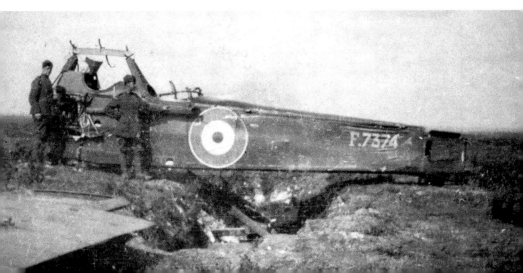

Capt C. R. Robbins was the pilot of C8406 that witnessed the plight of their colleagues Lts Strudwick and Weller and was able to alert nearby troops to render assistance. (M. O'Connor)

during a successful ammunition drop noted cyclists moving over open ground. However, during a contact patrol over Mametz Wood at 0915hrs FK8 F7374 was attacked by six enemy scouts. Lt Charles Strudwick and 2/Lt Adrian Weller did their best to fight them off but their aircraft was badly hit and both men were wounded. Charles Strudwick managed to maintain control but had to force land a couple of miles away at Maurepas. Their crash was seen by Capt Robbins and 2/Lt McNay from FK8 C8406 who was able to alert nearby troops. They were able to rescue the downed crew and both men were taken to a dressing station where their wounds were treated. However, German shelling then wrecked their aircraft.

Later in the day Mametz Wood was captured, a significant and emotional event and the following day, 26 August, the First Army struck east. By the end of the month it had taken the old Somme battlefield pushing back 35 German divisions in just ten days. The end of the war was now in sight.

The shooting down of Lt Strudwick's aircraft was witnessed by the crew of 35 Squadron FK8 C8406 that were flying nearby. (M. O'Connor)

# DOWN IN THE DESERT
# 16 September 1918

By the end of August 1918, the Palestine-based 144 Squadron commanded by Maj A. H. Peck was fully equipped with the de Havilland DH9. It formed part of 40 (Army) Wing and had two flights based at Junction Station, 15 miles west of Jerusalem with the third located further north at Haifa. Through much of early September in preparation for the coming offensive the RAF was attacking targets in the Ottoman rear areas with particular emphasis on the vital Hejaz railway. Also active behind the lines were the irregular Arab forces under Maj T. E. Lawrence conducting a raid deep into the desert to demolish sections of the Hejaz railway line. Gen Allenby's decisive final offensive was due to be launched on 19 September and the disruption to the Turkish communications by Lawrence and RAF air attacks were a key part of the preparations.

Raids by RAF bombers to support the Arabs were also mounted and on 16 September six DH9s of 144 Squadron set out from Junction Station to attack the important rail junction at Der'a in southern Syria, 56 miles south of Damascus.

DH9 C6293 '3' of 144 Squadron at Junction Station in September 1918. (J. M. Bruce)

Between them the six aircraft dropped five 112lb bombs and four dozen 20lb Cooper bombs onto the target and the sight of the aircraft bombing greatly boosted the morale of Lawrence's men. However, during the return flight of DH9 C6297 '3' flown by Lt T. L. Gitsham with 2/Lt G. C. H. Thomas as observer suffered a gradual failure of the unreliable Siddeley Puma engine. Eventually the engine seized and they had to force land the aircraft in the desert behind Ottoman lines. However, when landing on the rough surface the undercarriage broke off and the aircraft slid to a halt on its belly. Once it had stopped, Gitsham and Thomas got out of the aircraft as the other aircraft of the formation circled and they were able to wave showing that they were uninjured. They had also laid a circle of cloth as a signal to the other aircraft not to attempt a landing and conduct a rescue as the ground was too rough and stony.

Sadly, enemy troops had also seen their plight and a cavalry patrol soon appeared and the pair were quickly captured. The Turks then covered the aircraft with brushwood in an attempt to camouflage it. However, the returning crews had noted the position of the downed aircraft and the next day two Bristol Fighters from 1 Squadron Australian Flying Corps flew to the site and having identified the DH9 then dropped bombs that set it on fire. It was consumed by the flames and totally destroyed. Gitsham and Thomas were taken away by their Turkish captors but fortunately both later managed

Lt Gitsham and 2/Lt Thomas wave to their colleagues after successfully force-landing DH9 C6297 '3' on 16 September 1918. (Author's Collection)

The advance on the Allied right flank by Arab Northern Army under T. E. Lawrence was supported by RAF bombing. (S. James)

to escape. Thomas returned to British lines on 28 September and Gitsham followed a week later on 5 October.

The British offensive that developed as the Battle of Megiddo began as planned on the 19th. At 0630hrs five DH9s of 144 Squadron took off from Junction Station to attack the central telephone exchange at El Affule, several miles south of the town of Nazareth dropping four 112lb and 32 20lb bombs. The attack was repeated by eight more DH9s later in the day that completely destroyed the target. The squadron also bombed targets around Nablus. The Ottoman 7th Army was soon in retreat and several days later was trapped and largely destroyed by air attacks in Wadi al Far'a in a devastating demonstration of air power. A few days later the advance on Damascus began and on 30 October the Ottomans signed an armistice.

# RAID ON FORT ALEXANDROVSK
## 22 May 1919

After the end of WW1, elements of the fledgling Royal Air Force were committed in support of the anti-Bolshevik White Russian forces for operations over the Caspian Sea for which a seaplane base was established at Petrovsk on the west coast. No. 266 Squadron under Capt John Sadler was selected to fly the aircraft and to form the draft for service in south Russia and in early February 1919 it sailed to Batum on the Black Sea. From there the unit with its ten new Short Type 184 seaplanes was moved by

The officers of 266 Squadron in May 1919. Note the mixture of uniforms. Capt Sadler the CO is in the middle row, second from right. (via E. F. Cheesman)

For most of its time in the Caspian Sea 266 Squadron's Short Type 184s were embarked in the converted tanker HMS *Aladar Youssanoff* seen off Fort Alexandrovsk in mid-May 1919 with Short Type184s embarked. (R. Cronin)

train via Baku, eventually reaching Petrovsk on 18 March. The next month was then spent erecting and testing the aircraft. So as to fully support the Caspian Flotilla the tanker *Aladar Youssanoff* was converted to carry seaplanes and commissioned into the Royal Navy. She was declared ready for operations on 10 May despite communist-inspired strikes in the shipyard. Two days later she sailed with Shorts N9080 and N9082 embarked under the command of Lt Chiltern.

The target was Fort Alexandrovsk on the eastern shores of the Caspian that had been seized by the Bolsheviks and where much shipping was reported. HMS *Aladar Youssanoff* anchored off Chechen Is and on 14 May Capt Sadler and Lt Kingham flew a recce in N9080. The ship sailed that evening and the following day some ships were spotted off Fort Alexandrovsk though these quickly returned to harbour. After

Lts Morrison and Pratt cling to the wreckage of Short Type 184 N9079 after it had crashed soon after take-off on 20 May 1919. (G. S. Leslie)

a period of strong winds and rain, on the 17th both aircraft were prepared for an attack but both were damaged by the continued high winds. The ship then departed for Petrovsk where Short N9079 joined the repaired N9080 when she sailed again that evening. Reconnaissance revealed that the Bolsheviks had assembled eight destroyers,

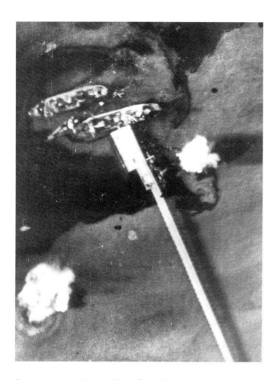

Bombs dropped from a Short Type 184 floatplane explode around Bolshevik ships, including the icebreaker *Caspi* at the end of the mole in Fort Alexandrovsk harbour on 22 May 1919. (R. Cronin)

five armed ships, 14 armed motorboats and two gunboats in Fort Alexandrovsk harbour.

Early on 20 May when 50 miles south of Fort Alexandrovsk *Aladar Youssanoff* launched the two Short seaplanes but after lifting off N9079 entered a climbing turn for the target and crashed in the sea. Fortunately, the bombs did not explode and 2/Lt Robert Morrison and Lt Henry Pratt were rescued unharmed. Short N9080 flown by 2/Lt Howard Thompson and Lt Frank Bicknell carried out a successful attack on the ships in the harbour dropping one 230lb, one 100lb and one 65lb bomb. Capt Sadler with Lt Kingham later flew N9080 for another attack, but contaminated fuel forced them to abandon the sortie. In fine weather, the following morning Sadler attempted another raid but the fuel contamination again forced an abandonment of the sortie. However, the rest of the Caspian squadron approached Fort Alexandrovsk and in a major engagement left a number of Bolshevik ships burning in the V-shaped harbour. As the force withdrew Sadler in N9080 flew a bombing attack on the guardship in the harbour.

On 22 May activity was confined to bombing by Short N9080 which throughout the day flew five bombing attacks on the harbour at Fort Alexandrovsk. Two were flown by Morrison and Pratt, the latter noting of one: "Three bombs 100ft to right of ships. Fired on various ships with MG. No AA." This crew later also bombed the pier. 2/Lt Thompson and Lt Bicknell were next off and claimed a hit on a Finn-class destroyer followed later by Sadler and Kingham who dropped their 230lb bomb between a destroyer and the icebreaker *Caspi* alongside a pier and both were later reported sunk. They also bombed and sank several small fishing boats. The Shorts'

Having carefully manoeuvred close to the ship a Short Type 184 is hooked up prior to hoisting aboard during operations in the Caspian Sea. (via E. F. Cheesman)

crews also reported sighting a number of sunken ships from the naval action the previous day.

After this carnage, early on the 23rd two Bolshevik destroyers were spotted and at 1030hrs Short Type 184 N9080 crewed by Capt Sadler with Lt Kingham as observer was launched and mounted an attack after which the destroyers departed to the north. However, the Short crew then headed for Fort Alexandrovsk where they bombed a large barge armed with a six-inch gun before returning to *Aladar Youssanoff*. However, a dense fog enveloped the area and the seaplane force-landed on the sea and eventually the aircraft sank leaving Sadler and Kingham to spend an uncomfortable 32 hours clinging to an upturned float before being picked up. Sadler wrote afterwards:

"Kingham and I clung to floats till 18.30 on the 24th when we were picked up by HMS *Asia* (Lt. Wilson) 20 miles south-west of Cape Orlok. I had given up hope and was in a pretty rotten state. *Asia* very decent, gave us hot drinks, hot bath, grub and bed."

Nonetheless, the successful actions over the preceding days forced the Bolsheviks to evacuate their warships back to the River Volga above Astrakhan leaving three barges and a dozen other vessels sunk at Fort Alexandrovsk harbour. The success was further buoyed by news that the Red naval commander had been replaced and shot!

## PART 2

# WORLD WAR II

# *WATUSSI* INCIDENT
# 2 December 1939

The outbreak of war in September 1939 found the South African Air Force (SAAF) lacking modern equipment so the 18 Junkers Ju 86Zs of South African Airways (SAA) were impressed for military service. Their conversion for military use included the fitting of external bomb racks, additional fuel capacity and installing a dorsal gun position and a ventral turret. As the security of the sea-lanes around the coastline of the Union was the priority, four squadrons were formed at coastal locations, each equipped with three Ju 86s with most of the pilots being ex-SAA. Initially the aircraft continued to wear their civilian registrations with the addition of SAAF roundels. These sorties also carried a naval officer as part of the crew though the aircraft had few navigation aids and no life jackets or parachutes!

Based at Wingfield near Cape Town under Maj J. M. B. Botes was 15 Squadron equipped with Ju 86Zs ZS-AGE 'Louis Trichardt', ZS-AJK 'Hendrik Swellengrebel' and ZS-ALN 'Sir Hercules Robinson'. The squadron was initially tasked with sea

At Wingfield and still in its SAA colours Junkers Ju 86Z ZS-AGE was the first SAAF aircraft to engage the *Watussi*. (SAAF)

reconnaissance out to 65 miles from the coast but this was later increased out to 140 miles. Early operations for the Ju 86s centred on searches for the pocket battleship *Admiral Graf Spee*. Then on 1 December the Ju 86 units were rationalised and reorganised, with 15 and 16 Squadrons amalgamating to form 32 Squadron becoming respectively A and B Flights. The very next day success crowned the efforts of the SAAF's Junkers crews.

On 22 November, the 9,500-ton Deutsche Ost-Afrika liner *Watussi* which had been bottled up in the Mozambique port of Lourenço Marques (now Maputo) sailed for South America carrying a crew of 49 and 155 expatriate German passengers. Shortly after 0800hrs on 2 December, Capt H. G. B. Boshoff and crew in Ju 86Z ZS-AGE left Wingfield on a patrol. Two hours later when on their final leg and the aircraft was 70 miles south of Cape Point, 2/Lt Driver, the co-pilot, spotted a ship that was identified by the RN observer Lt McEwan as the *Watussi*. Reporting the sighting by wireless the ship was signalled and ordered to head for Cape Town, though initially the *Watussi*'s master, Capt Stamer, ignored the Aldis lamp signal. To persuade him otherwise, Boshoff ordered a burst of gunfire across the bows then a 112lb bomb was dropped and it exploded in the sea close to the ship. After a second bomb was dropped the vessel changed course but soon afterwards fuel shortage forced Boshoff to withdraw after which the ship resumed its original course.

At 1230hrs Capt D. B. Raubenheimer in Junkers ZS-ALN took off and when it arrived overhead contacted the *Watussi* that once more altered course for Cape Town,

Smoke pours from the blazing hulk of the *Watussi* off the South African coast on the afternoon of 2 December. (SAAF)

Flown by Maj Botes, Ju 86Z ZS-AJK arrived over the *Watussi* just in time to see the lifeboats being lowered. (SAAF)

though only making a speed of two to three knots. Warned to increase speed or be attacked, *Watussi* then began steaming at eight knots and hoisted the German flag. A third Ju 86, ZS-AJK, flown by the squadron CO Maj J. M. B. Botes took off at 1415hrs and arriving on scene an hour later saw that the ship's lifeboats had been swung out, but were unmanned. Ten minutes later the ship suddenly stopped and the lifeboats were lowered as smoke was seen pouring from *Watussi*'s after-hold. Capt Stamer had set fire to his ship. Despite warning bursts of machine-gun fire from the Ju 86, *Watussi*'s crew continued to abandon ship and within a few minutes it was completely enveloped in flames. Having refuelled and returned to the scene, Boshoff saw that the ship had by then developed a significant list. Guided in by the Junkers the cruiser HMS *Sussex* arrived at 1800hrs and picked up the survivors though requests from the enthusiastic airmen to bomb *Watussi*'s blazing hulk were refused. Instead as darkness began to fall, the battlecruiser HMS *Renown* sank the liner by gunfire.

This was the SAAF's first action of the war and despite the frustration of not bringing in the ship to port it was seen as a great success. In his report, Maj Botes wrote:

> "I regret very much that we were unable to bring the ship into port as a prize, and I feel that had we been permitted to carry out our original intentions of destroying the lifeboats whilst still stowed this would have been achieved."

# BRIEF ENCOUNTER
# 19 December 1939

The declaration of war in September 1939 forced the Royal Air Force to use all its available coastal aircraft in patrolling the maritime approaches to Britain in an effort to protect shipping from German submarines. The shortage of more modern aircraft like the Short Sunderland and delays in the promised SARO Lerwick led to a number of antiquated biplane flying boats like the Supermarine Stranraer and SARO London remaining in use. The latter equipped 240 Squadron under Wg Cdr R. H. Carter based at Sullom Voe in the Shetland Islands for patrols over northern waters between Norway and Iceland. Often flown in the most atrocious weather conditions these patrols occasionally encountered patrolling Luftwaffe reconnaissance aircraft that presented an additional hazard.

The first such encounter was on 29 November when Flt Lt McConnell's crew flying London K5263 was attacked by a Dornier Do 18 flying boat which approached

The exposed nose gun position of the SARO London from which the gunner fired on the He 111 with his Lewis gun. (Author's Collection)

London II K5258/BN-H of 240 Squadron at Sullom Voe in mid-December 1939 after the action against a Do 18. A ship had dragged anchor in a gale and ended among aircraft. (Wg Cdr H. C. Bailey)

the biplane from astern with its front gunner opening fire at about 200 yards as McConnell put his aircraft into a climbing turn. A slightly bizarre combat then ensued with the London's gunners returning fire as the Dornier dived to within a few feet of the sea and zigzagged off to the south. Some 20 minutes later the Dornier, thought to be '6K+FH' of 1./Ku.Fl.Gr.406 approached once more but again McConnell turned the London towards it but neither of the lumbering aircraft were able to gain an advantage and eventually went their own ways. While the London was undamaged, the Dornier had been hit so limped away and force-landed in Norway. The squadron's next encounter with an enemy aircraft that came almost three weeks later had a tragically different outcome.

At 0800hrs on 19 December 23-year-old Flt Lt Vincent Pam eased London K5258/BN-H off Sullom Voe's choppy waters and headed north for a patrol towards the Faroe Islands with his eight-man crew. About two and a half hours later when on a south-westerly course at 1,000 feet above the choppy sea the crew spotted a Heinkel He 111 heading in a northerly direction. Pam immediately called his crew to action stations and turned away to starboard as well as diving towards the surface. However, the Heinkel's crew from KG 26 out on a shipping reconnaissance had spotted the elderly biplane and turned to attack. The operational diary of 240 Squadron recounted the subsequent events:

"The E/A approached and flew across the London's bow, diving from port to starboard, opening fire at about 800 yards above the London. The London then commenced to climb towards the clouds, and when at about 1,500 feet the Heinkel came back from starboard to port firing more bursts and killing the first pilot. The London returned fire with all three guns, firing in all 250 rounds. The air gunners state that hits were made in the starboard engine of the E/A."

Five minutes after Pam had been hit the co-pilot, Fg Off R. E. Hunter made what was noted as a particularly skilful landing on rough seas so that the unfortunate Pam could be treated. Sadly, his wounds were too severe and he died about ten minutes after they had alighted. Fortunately, the Heinkel, possibly because it had itself been damaged, did not interfere further and had left the area. Some 30 minutes after landing Hunter then took the London off the water and the crew flew it back to Sullom Voe. Vincent Pam's death came as a severe blow to the close-knit squadron as he was considered 'an outstanding officer and an excellent pilot'. He was buried in Lerwick New Cemetery three days later with honours from the RAF and RN and a detachment from the Argyll and Sutherland Highlanders.

The London's brief encounter with the enemy had sadly been a deadly one but the incident was recorded in a remarkable photograph taken from the cockpit of the Heinkel that showed Vincent Pam's London crossing the nose in a right-hand turn, exchanging fire with its enemy.

London K5258/BN-H of 240 Squadron turns across the nose of the Heinkel He 111 that was encountered with deadly results north of Shetland on 19 December 1939. (via J. D. Oughton)

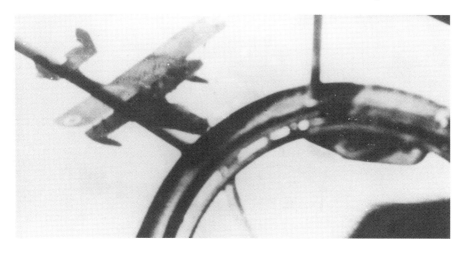

# OUT OF THEIR TIME
## 27 May 1940

The ferocious German assault against France and the Low Countries that opened on 10 May 1940 soon had the British Expeditionary Force trapped against the Channel coast. The main perimeter was around Dunkirk from where a massive evacuation soon began, but there was also a significant garrison in the port of Calais. So desperate did the situation become that even the most unlikely types were pressed into action, among them the obsolete Hawker Hector army co-operation biplanes. At the time of the German offensive 613 (County of Manchester) Squadron under Sqn Ldr Alan Anderson was at Odiham as part of 22 (Army Cooperation) Group, which was in the throes of re-equipping with the Lysander but still had one flight flying the obsolescent Hectors. On 20 May, the squadron sent a detachment to Lympne to provide maintenance and servicing facilities to several Lysander squadrons which had such a torrid time in France. Plt Off John Rowland recalled: "It seemed that things were not going too well for us but as we were equipped with Hectors we did not think that there would be any call for us." Events were to prove him wrong.

This rare flying view of a 613 Squadron Hector at the time of the operations over Calais gives an idea of the sight of the aircraft in formation. (613 Squadron Association via R. A. Scholefield)

Plt Off Paddy Barthropp flew on the first Hector operation and whose gunner got into trouble for hurling his broken gun at the Germans. (P. Lake)

Former Cranwell cadet Plt Off John Rowland flew a Hector to Calais on 27 May barely two weeks after his first flight on the type. (RAF College Cranwell)

On 24 May HQ 22 Group ordered that all the squadron's Hectors should be fitted with universal bomb racks and at 1530hrs the aircraft left for Hawkinge, just across the Channel from the cauldrons of Dunkirk and Calais. Plt Off Edmonds in K9713 returned early due to a lack of fuel pressure and the remainder came back at 1900hrs owing to bombs at Hawkinge being the incorrect size for the Hectors' bomb racks. After a period on standby the Hector flight came to readiness at first light on 26 May when Sqn Ldr Anderson flying K9706 with Plt Off Wesson as his gunner led K8111 (Plt Off Bernard Brown/LAC Brown), K8127 (Plt Off Al Edy/ Plt Off 'Tiger' Houghton), K9727 (Plt Off Stewart/LAC Conache), K9781 (Plt Off Paddy Barthropp/AC1 MacKinnon) and K8108 (Plt Off Gore/AC1 Leathen) down to Hawkinge once more where they arrived 30 minutes later. Each was loaded with a pair of 120lb GP bombs before the Hectors took off in two vics at 0950hrs to attack a battery of large field guns four miles south-west of Calais on the outskirts of Peuplingues. Anderson's section approached from the north and carried out dive-bombing attacks dropping their bombs as a salvo. He afterwards described the Hector's combat debut:

"I saw bursts from my own bombs, one dropping within the coppice detailed as the target, and one in open country 150 yards south of it. The gun positions were difficult to identify owing to camouflage and heavy AA fire was encountered."

The other section led by Plt Off Gore approached from the east and from out of the smoke haze hanging over Calais carried out similar attacks while Plt Off Barthropp dived down to strafe some German troops. All the Hectors returned independently.

The deteriorating situation in Calais meant an airdrop of supplies by Lysander was arranged for the following morning with the bomb-carrying Hectors and RN

Swordfish providing the escort. Plt Off John Rowland said: "Our task was to fly three Hectors each side of Calais and create as much of a diversion as we could by dropping our bombs and firing our guns at anything we could see."

Thus, at 0945hrs on 27 May, having again bombed up at Hawkinge, Sqn Ldr Anderson once again flying K9706 with Plt Off Wesson led K8127 (Plt Off Al Edy/LAC Rushworth), K8116 (Plt Off Jenkyns/LAC Brown), K9781 (Flt Lt Gus Weston/Plt Off 'Tiger' Houghton), K9727 (Plt Off Stewart/Cpl Bickley) and K8108 (Plt Off John Rowland/LAC Conacher). The six Hectors set out and flew across the Channel at 1,500 feet on a beautiful clear morning with little cloud and light winds. Approaching Calais they divided into two sections – Anderson's trio flew to the south side of the town whilst Flt Lt Weston led his section to the north.

They dived in attacks on the anti-aircraft posts around Calais with bombs and machine-gun fire. Under this cover the large Lysander formation flew in and dropped the supplies, with the Hectors continuing attacks to cover them whilst they did so. The whole operation was successfully carried out and several machine-gun posts were put out of action. However, they did not escape unscathed as K8116/ZR-X was hit by anti-aircraft fire and unable to maintain height crashed into Shakespeare Cliff, Dover killing 25-year-old LAC Reg Brown and seriously injuring Plt Off Reg Jenkyns.

The other Hectors returned safely to Odiham with 613 Squadron having suffered its first casualties on an aircraft that was truly out of its time.

Having been hit by ground fire over Calais on 27 May Hector K8116 /ZR-X crashed at Dover killing the gunner and injuring the pilot. (J. Beedle)

# GET YER 'ANDS UP!
# 8 July 1940

At Schiphol airfield near Amsterdam early on the morning of Monday 8 July Hptm Karl Rohloff the Staffelkapitän of 9./KG 4 briefed his crew of Uffz Heinz Oechler, Uffz Artur Kuhnapfel and Uffz George Abel for a search off the east coast of England looking for any coastal shipping. They took off in Junkers Ju 88A-1 W/nr 3094 '5J+AT' and headed west towards Sunderland.

At about 1130hrs (British time) the crew was flying intermittently in cloud at 15,000ft some miles off the Yorkshire coast when a northbound convoy was spotted. However, unknown to them they were being tracked by one of the then secret Chain Home RDF (radar) stations whose coverage at the height of the Junkers extended well out to sea. From Catterick a pair of Spitfire Is of 41 Squadron flown by

A pair of Spitfire Is of 41 Squadron at the time of the engagement with Karl Rohloff's Ju 88.
(J. D. R. Rawlings)

Fg Off Tony Lovell in P9429 with Sgt Jack Allison as No. 2 had been scrambled. Off Scarborough they spotted Karl Rohloff's aircraft and promptly swept in to attack with their .303in bullets riddling the bomber, putting the starboard engine out of action. Their fire also hit the cabin, wounding George Abel the gunner. Sgt Allison described the attack:

> "Fg Off Lovell attacked and I saw a large piece of what appeared to be a portion of the tail fall off. I gave two bursts when the e/a was amongst the clouds. I then saw Fg Off Lovell following it again but lost him in clouds. Three Hurricanes were circling round at the time."

Reaching the sanctuary of cloud, Karl Rohloff then managed to evade the Spitfires but his aircraft had been badly hit. Realising that the aircraft would not make it back to the Netherlands the crew jettisoned the four 250kg bombs and turned towards land.

The three Hurricanes Allison had seen were of Green Section, 249 Squadron led by Fg Off Denis Parnall flying P3615/GN-D with Plt Off Hugh Beazley in P3055/GN-W and Sgt Alistair Main in P2995. The crippled bomber was heading south about 15 miles north of Flamborough Head when the Hurricanes spotted it. As Denis Parnall was positioning his section to attack he noted the Spitfires breaking

A Hurricane I of 249 Squadron scrambling at the time of the 8 July action. (R. G. A. Barclay via G. Barclay)

away. Rohloff desperately evaded by flying slowly, executing several stall turns as the Hurricanes approached. Parnall described his attack: "I fired a nine-second burst, commencing at 350 yards, breaking away at 40 yards." He did not note any return fire before Hugh Beazley followed him in. He wrote of his attack:

"After a two-second burst, enemy stall-turned to right and I had to go into firm pitch to pull up and follow him round. Enemy entered cloud but I caught him coming out the other side and got in a burst before he again turned sharply to the left, diving slightly. I again opened fire as he straightened out. I observed white streaks coming past the starboard wing. I ceased firing as he dived into cloud again."

Although he did not see the Junkers again, he noted a strong smell of burning metal as the Hurricane entered cloud.

Despite becoming enveloped in cloud, Rohloff's crippled Junkers gained little respite as Alistair Main continued the assault: "I gave a short burst before No. 2 broke away. Following the E/A through cloud I came out to find myself on his tail, gave a burst of three to four seconds." By this time both of the bomber's engines were on fire so he broke off to re-join the rest of the section. Struggling to retain control of the doomed aircraft, Rohloff ordered his crew to bale out but no sooner had they

The shattered remains of Karl Rohloff's Ju 88 are examined by British personnel where it came down near the village of Aldbrough in East Yorkshire. (via M. Postlethwaite)

The fin of '5T+AT' sits in the field where it came down on 8 July. (via M. Postlethwaite)

The tip of a propeller blade of 5J+AT showing a .303in bullet hole survives to this day and sits in the author's study. (Author)

exited the burning bomber than he lost control and it fell away to explode between Aldbrough and Crossmere Hill, a dozen miles north-east of Hull, close to the seaside town of Hornsea. Its gallant pilot was still aboard. It was 1142hrs.

The three surviving Germans descended by parachute with one landing in a field at East Carlton Farm where he was spotted by the farmer's wife, Mrs Eveline Cardwell, who also served as a tea lady with the Women's Voluntary Service (WVS). Although unarmed she was undaunted and as the injured German airman approached she beckoned him to raise his arms with a no-nonsense shout of 'Get your 'ands up' before disarming him of his pistol. Eveline then sent a farm worker to summon the Local Defence Volunteers (later the Home Guard). This airman and his two colleagues who were quickly captured were then taken into captivity.

Eveline Cardwell's pluck impressed even Winston Churchill and on 1 August she was presented with the British Empire Medal by HM the King.

# BLUNTING SEALION
## 15 September 1940

Following the fall of France in June 1940, after his overtures had been rejected, on 16 July Hitler issued Führer Directive No 16 for the invasion of Britain – Operation *Seelöwe* (Sealion). The directive stated that the aim was '...to eliminate the English Motherland as a base from which the war against Germany can be continued, and, if necessary, to occupy the country completely.' During July Churchill became increasingly concerned at the prospect and warned that the priority for bombing might become enemy harbours and shipping rather than the German aircraft industry. Reconnaissance of possible ports of embarkation was stepped up and this revealed an increase in shipping movements including shallow-draught barges that would be necessary for an invasion. Thus, in early September Bomber Command was ordered

Hampden I L4095/OL-R bearing the scars of flak damage received over Antwerp during the attack on 15 September when it was flown by Plt Off Cook and his crew. (via M. Postlethwaite)

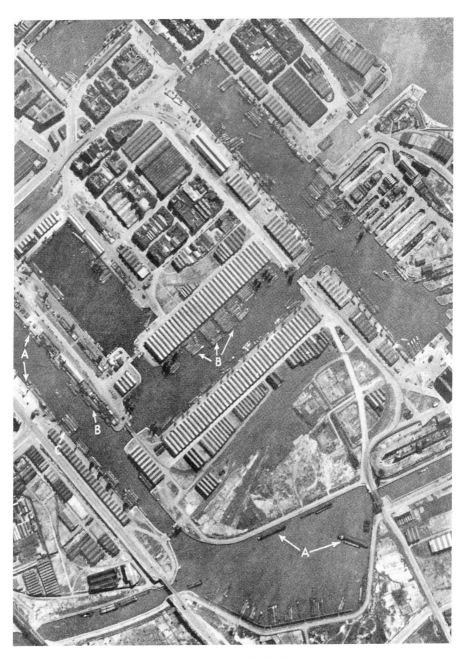

The port of Antwerp is packed with invasion barges marked in this reconnaissance photo taken in mid-September. (Author's Collection)

to concentrate most of its attacks on shipping in potential ports of embarkation in Belgium and France for an invasion force.

On 7 September, the presence of increasing numbers of barges in the Channel ports resulted in an 'invasion imminent' alert. Shortly after 2000hrs that evening five Hampdens of 83 Squadron lifted off from Scampton to attack the Belgian port of Ostend, Flt Lt Bird for example seeing showers of sparks among the barges. Four more of the squadron's Hampdens led by Flt Lt Jamie Pitcairn-Hill flying P1193 attacked Ostend the following night. All bombed successfully with Fg Off Guy Gibson flying X2097 seeing three of his bombs burst in the dockyard whilst from the cockpit of P4402 Plt Off Harwood observed his bombs bursting in some buildings and starting fires; all the crews attacked in the face of intense anti-aircraft fire, however.

Calais and Ostend were attacked on the night of 11 September and 83 Squadron then did not operate for several days but it was evident that German preparations were reaching their peak when over 100 barges were seen in Boulogne and 136 at Calais. There were over 600 more positioned at Antwerp which were the target for 35 bombers on the night of the 15th.

Shortly after 2100hrs that night 15 Hampdens of 83 Squadron began taking off on its largest attack of the war thus far. In indifferent weather nine of them bombed the docks and town at Antwerp whilst three others bombed Flushing and Dunkirk

The burned underside of the Hampden bears grim testimony to the intensity of the flames braved by Sgt Hannah. (RAF Scampton)

Sgt John Hannah (left) was awarded the VC for his courage during the attack on Antwerp on 15 September while Plt Off Clare Connor (right) received the DFC. (RAF Scampton)

instead. Bombing from just 800ft, Fg Off Guy Gibson saw several big explosions result and he also bombed another barge up river. Plt Off Harwood made a glide attack hitting barges and wharves on the Bassin Lefebre whilst in P2097 Flt Lt Bird made a dive attack and saw his bombs explode among the barges.

The flak over Antwerp was intense and L4095/OL-R was hit in the port-wing root, though Plt Off Cook flew safely back to Scampton. However, just after releasing its bombs P1355/OL-P flown by Plt Off Clare Connor was caught by the searchlights, hit by flak and set on fire. The rear fuselage swiftly became an inferno forcing the air gunner to bale out. Connor said afterwards: "I could see we were in trouble when I saw the reflection of flames in my windscreen, the flames were getting very close to the back of my neck." Despite being surrounded by flames and with his cockpit floor melting, Sgt John Hannah the wireless operator fought the flames with two small fire extinguishers before beating at the flames with his logbook and finally his hands. He succeeded in putting the flames out but the heat was making the ammunition explode and he disposed of them through the gaping hole in the fuselage. Crawling painfully forward he discovered that the observer had also been forced to bale out so he then assisted Plt Off Connor with bringing the aircraft back to Scampton. Badly burned, the 18-year-old Hannah was taken to hospital for treatment to his injuries and soon afterwards he was awarded the Victoria Cross; Plt Off Connor was awarded the DFC.

The Hampdens of 83 Squadron continued attacks on the invasion barges that were assembled in the Channel ports such as Dunkirk that was bombed on 20 September, though by the end of the month it was assessed that the risk of invasion had receded. It was estimated that ten per cent of the assembled invasion shipping had been destroyed; Bomber Command then returned to German targets.

# A CHRISTMAS DEBUT
# 25 December 1940

With the Battle of Britain at its height, in September 1940 804 Naval Air Squadron under Lt Cdr John Cockburn was based at Hatston on Orkney with eight obsolescent Sea Gladiators. It was part of the Fighter Command Order of Battle for the defence of the Scapa Flow naval base. On 7 September, the squadron received its first two Grumman G-36As that had been taken over from French contracts and given the name 'Martlet' in Royal Navy service. Although fitted with French instrumentation they were nonetheless a step change from the biplanes and much more capable of intercepting Luftwaffe reconnaissance aircraft which were regularly appearing near Orkney. By mid-October 804 Squadron was fully equipped though frustratingly saw nothing of the Luftwaffe. Nonetheless, the tubby little Grummans were the only US-built fighters to see service during the Battle of Britain.

The nearest two aircraft are Martlet Is BJ562/A flown by Lt Carver and BJ561/S7-L flown by Sub-Lt Parke who shot down the Ju 88 over Orkney on Christmas Day 1940. (R. H. P. Carver)

Ltn Karl Schipp who with his crew unexpectedly spent Christmas Day in Orkney. (Orkney Library)

During the squadron's work-up period several aircraft were wrecked in accidents, including one when Sub-Lt Jimmy Sleigh crash-landed at Skeabrea on 7 November. Shortly afterwards Lt Cdr Bryan Kendall took command and by Christmas his squadron was fully operational, sharing responsibility for the defence of the naval base with locally based RAF fighter squadrons.

At their base at Schiphol near Amsterdam on the evening of 24 December 1940 Ltn Karl Schipp and his crew celebrated *Heiligabend* (Christmas Eve), probably enjoying a traditional German meal of fish and potatoes. They belonged to 3 (F)/122, a long-range reconnaissance unit, equipped with the fast Junkers Ju 88A and the following morning the crew was briefed for a mission to Britain. They were tasked to photograph the anchorage of the Royal Navy's Home Fleet at Scapa Flow in the Orkney Islands off the north coast of Scotland. With Fw H. Schreiber, Uffz H. Sportl and Obgefr K. Rotter, Schipp left Schiphol in mid-morning in Junkers Ju 88A W/nr 535 '4N+AL' and set course across the North Sea for Orkney, some 450 miles distant.

The RAF air defence radar stations had been finely honed during the Luftwaffe's attacks over the previous months and as Karl Schipp's Ju 88 crossed the North Sea it was detected and tracked. As a single aircraft, it was assessed as being on a reconnaissance and its likely destination identified correctly by the sector controller as Scapa Flow. Eventually the sector controller scrambled fighters to intercept the intruder and shortly after 1400hrs six Martlets of 804 Squadron were scrambled from Hatston. The two Martlets of 'Red' Section comprised Lt Rodney Carver flying BJ562/A leading BJ561/S7-L flown by Sub-Lt Tom Parke and under the direction of the radar controller they climbed for height.

High over the islands they sighted the Junkers and closed to engage the intruder. The Martlet pilots attacked in turn and the fire from their .50 in Browning machine guns hit the Junkers' tailplane, the radiator in the starboard engine and severed an oil pipe in the port engine. With damage to both engines, and his air gunner badly wounded, the long return flight over the North Sea was not possible and so Karl Schipp opted to put down on land rather than ditch. By now the two fighters had pulled away as

Sub-Lt Tom Parke who was one of the successful Martlet pilots. (Author's Collection)

Ltn Schipp descended and skilfully landed his crippled aircraft wheels up on fields at Sandwick on the west side of mainland Orkney, four miles to the north of Stromness. Two members of the Home Guard, local farmer Thomas Harcus and his son Leslie, were quickly on the scene and arrested the German crew before they could set fire to their aircraft; they also gave first aid to the wounded air gunner. Their captives were quickly taken over by Royal Navy personnel and very soon were transferred to the mainland.

Having watched their victim go down, Carver and Parke then returned to Hatston cock-a-hoop. Not only had they claimed 804 Squadron's first victory but had also claimed the first of countless victories for the tubby Grumman fighter. This was also the penultimate German aircraft to fall over Britain during the momentous year of 1940 and, to their undoubted chagrin Karl Schipp's crew celebrated their *Weihnachten* (Christmas Day) in Orkney.

Junkers Ju 88A '4N+AL' of 3 (F)/122 that crash-landed at Sandwick, Orkney after attack by the two Martlets. (R. H. P. Carver)

# ERITREAN ADVENTURE
# 25 March 1941

The first significant British success against the Axis during WW2 came with the fall of Eritrea during the campaign against the Italians in East Africa. The crucial battle of this part of the campaign was fought at Keren, an extraordinarily strong and well-protected natural mountain fortress. Indeed, it was possibly the toughest natural fortress to be assaulted during the entire war. All available RAF and SAAF assets, including the Vickers Wellesley bombers of 47 and 223 Squadrons, supported the British and Indian forces that launched their assault against a numerically superior Italian force on 15 March 1941.

From its HQ in the Sudanese capital, Khartoum, 47 Squadron was detached forward to Agordat in central Eritrea to support these operations. During the first day of the attack the sailplane-like Wellesleys dropped around 19 tons of bombs on the Italian defences in a series of shuttle raids. To help counter these raids the following

With both cockpits open against the high temperatures a 47 Squadron Wellesley approaches the rugged hills around Keren during a raid on the Italian defences. (47 Squadron Records)

day, 16 March, the Italians moved all available aircraft of the Regia Aeronautica, which included a dozen Fiat CR.42 fighters, forward to Dessie. The Wellesleys of both squadrons flew 40 sorties during the day but the Italians fought back and one 47 Squadron formation was attacked by five of the CR.42s. M.Ilo Aroldo Soffritti, an ace with nine victories, shot down Wellesley K8527 flown by Plt Off Leuchars and he was the only one of the crew who managed to bale out. The attacks continued throughout the next day, the bombing having a considerable effect, particularly on the morale of the Italian colonial units. However, at dawn the following day, 18 March, the Fiats struck back with an effective strafing attack on Agordat which amongst other damage destroyed one of 47 Squadron's aircraft. Its wreckage joined that of four others in what was fast becoming a 'Wellesley graveyard'. At Keren the British and Indian troops continued their advance against the Italian positions on the 22nd when the key Marda Pass was taken. However, the Italian defence was dogged and fighting was stiff so progress over the rugged terrain was slow.

The Battle of Keren reached its climax on 25 March during which 47 Squadron's Wellesleys flew a further 16 sorties over the front with Wellesleys flown by Sgt Keith and Plt Off Collis being first off at 0300hrs. The squadron's final raid of the day took off at 1400hrs and comprised four Wellesleys. Flying K7715/KU-H was Plt Off Walter Kennedy with Sgt Turner as observer and gunner Sgt German. This aircraft was one of a number of Wellesleys to have been fitted with a long 'glasshouse' canopy over the space between the two cockpits. As the bombers approached Keren they were attacked by Fiat CR.42s of the 412ª Squadriglia that vigorously pressed home their attacks. Two of the Fiats concentrated on K7715 against which Sgt German gallantly tried to defend the bomber with his single drum-fed Vickers gun. However, he was hit and severely wounded by the Italian fire, before another burst then set the aircraft's port wing on fire close to the fuselage. Turner attempted to treat Douglas German's wounds, though these meant that the injured man was unable to bale out. In a desperate attempt to put out the flames and thus save his gunner, Walter Kennedy put the Wellesley into a near vertical dive. This fortunately caused the slipstream to blow the fire out and also allowed him to escape from his tormentors. However, the aircraft was badly damaged with much of the fabric having been burned off exposing the Wellesley's geodetic wing structure. Nonetheless, Kennedy managed to fly the damaged bomber back to Agordat where he carried out a successful crash landing.

Sadly, despite the best efforts and considerable courage of Plt Off Kennedy and Sgt Turner, Douglas German succumbed to his injuries the following day; the young Scot was buried at Keren War Cemetery.

Photographs taken the day after the action show Plt Off Walter Kennedy surveying the damaged Wellesley I K7715/KU-H after his Eritrean adventure. The damage, as well as the Wellesley's extended canopy and geodetic construction, are readily apparent. (47 Squadron Records)

The following day British and Indian troops cleared the final roadblock. That night Italian troops began withdrawing and Keren fell on 27 March. For his courage and performance during the battle, shortly afterwards Plt Off Walter Kennedy received the DFC, his citation noting that he had been:

"Attacked by two fighters during bombing run, set on fire, air gunner seriously wounded so did not abandon a/c. He partially put fire out and decided not to land at ALG in order to get gunner to medical care so returned to base and made a difficult landing."

# EYEWITNESS
# 24 May 1941

The naval engagement in the Denmark Strait between the German battleship *Bismarck* and heavy cruiser *Prinz Eugen* and a British squadron early on 24 May 1941 resulted in an explosion and the loss of the battlecruiser HMS *Hood*. From a shadowing Sunderland of 201 Squadron, L5798/ZM-Z flying from Iceland, Flt Lt R. J. Vaughn, the captain, was an eyewitness to the catastrophe and his report graphically describes the loss of HMS *Hood*:

"At 0537 hrs. on 24.5.41 a county-class cruiser was sighted steering a course of 240°T at an estimated speed of 28 kts. and at the same time gunfire was seen well ahead. As we closed, two columns, each of two ships in line ahead, were steering on parallel courses at an estimated range of 12 miles between columns. Heavy gunfire was being exchanged and the leading ship of the port column was on fire in two places, one being at the base of the bridge superstructure and the other further aft. In spite of these large conflagrations she appeared to be firing from at least one turret forward and aft. (This ship was found afterwards to be "HOOD".)

Sunderland I L5798/ZM-Z of 201 Squadron at anchor shortly before the incident. (G. M. Smith)

"At this juncture no engaged ships had been identified and I instructed the pilot to proceed towards the starboard column of ships. The second ship of this line (BISMARCK) [sic] was making a considerable amount of smoke which appeared to come from near the mainmast on the port side. Oil was also escaping and leaving a broad streak in the water behind her.

HMS *Hood* blows up in the Denmark Strait soon after dawn on 24 May 1941, an event witnessed by the Sunderland crew. (US Naval Historical Center)

"As we approached the two ships were identified as enemy and a first sighting report was made at 0610 hrs. Immediately prior to this an explosion was noticed on the burning ship of the port column (HOOD) and at the same time we came under AA fire from the enemy, and were forced to take cloud cover at 2,500ft. On emerging from cloud some five minutes later, the HOOD had almost completely disappeared and only one part of the bow was showing. The second ship of this line then fired a salvo which fell short and slightly ahead of the second enemy ship and immediately afterwards reversed course after having laid a light smoke screen. The second enemy (BISMARCK) then fired a salvo at the ship which had reversed course (later identified as PRINCE OF WALES) and this was a very near miss, with perhaps one hit near the stern.

"This was the most accurate I had observed during the action, the previous bursts from the enemy appearing to be well ahead, but with range correct and those from our units seemed to be either under or over, although in most cases line appeared to be too good.

"The leading ship (PRINZ EUGEN) of the enemy line had also been firing and the salvos also fell well ahead of our leading ship but range again appeared to be correct. After emerging from cloud we flew over the wreckage of the sunken warship, observing

*Bismarck* firing on HMS *Prince of Wales* in the Denmark Strait on 24 May 1941. (US Naval Historical Center)

one large red raft and a considerable amount of wreckage amidst a huge patch of oil. From the height we were flying, no survivors could actually be seen."

At 0650hrs the Sunderland crew transmitted a vital report: "Enemy course 220 true. 30 knots. No fire but *Bismarck* losing fuel."

It was largely based on this report and those from shadowing cruisers that the Admiralty assessed that *Bismarck* would abandon the operation and attempt to reach a German or French port. The RN dispositions were set accordingly. *Bismarck* had indeed been hit three times on the port side by fire from HMS *Prince of Wales*. The first shell hit below the waterline but exploded against the armoured belt whilst the third passed through a boat and caused little damage. However, the second 14in shell hit the bow just above the waterline above the armoured belt and passed through without exploding, leaving a 1½-metre diameter hole in the bows. The hits on *Bismarck's* bow caused significant flooding of some compartments, resulting in her shipping about 2,000 tons of seawater. However, more seriously it meant that around 1,000 tons of fuel oil had been rendered unusable.

Whilst it remained seaworthy, the ship's top speed was reduced to 28 knots so as to ease pressure on internal bulkheads. She also had a 9° list to port and was 3° down by the bow that at times exposed the blades of the starboard propeller screw. She was therefore not ideally placed to continue operations in the unpredictable weather of the North Atlantic. Thus, later in the day Adm Lütjens informed HQ Navy Group West that, due to fuel shortage, he was to proceed with *Bismarck* directly to St Nazaire on the French Atlantic coast thus setting in train the hunt that resulted in her destruction.

*Bismarck* clearly down by the bows and leaking fuel, a situation accurately reported by the Sunderland crew. (US Naval Historical Center)

# DAYLIGHT TO BREST
# 24 July 1941

On 22 March 1941 the German battlecruisers *Scharnhorst* and *Gneisenau* docked in the French port of Brest after their foray into the Atlantic during which they had destroyed over 115,000 tons of shipping. Six days later a photo-reconnaissance of the docks at Brest confirmed their presence so they immediately became a priority target for RAF bombers; the first attack was made on the night of 30/31 March. Two months later they were joined by the heavy cruiser *Prinz Eugen* though after a series

A reconnaissance photo of the German battlecruisers in Brest at the time of the July attack. (90 Squadron Records)

SCHARNHORST
AND
GNEISENAU.

Wg Cdr MacDougall the CO (right) participated in the 24 July attack dropping his bombs across Brest harbour. (90 Squadron Records)

of attacks *Scharnhorst* was moved 200 miles south to La Pallice and a large tanker covered with camouflage netting was left in its berth at Brest.

At the same time the Boeing Fortress I had been introduced to RAF service with 90 Squadron at Polebrook under Wg Cdr Jeffrey MacDougall to begin high-altitude daylight bombing exploiting the aircraft's excellent performance at height and the much-vaunted Sperry bombsight.

After two abortive attacks on Germany 90 Squadron was ordered to participate in a heavy daylight attack on the German capital ships in Brest on 24 July. Three Fortresses each armed with four 1,100lb bombs were prepared with AN523/WP-D flown by Sqn Ldr Andy McLaren and AN529/WP-C by Flt Lt Alex Mathieson taking off at 1120hrs with Wg Cdr MacDougall following in AN530/WP-F ten minutes later. In the clear skies the three Fortresses climbed steadily into the stratosphere. They flew to Brest unhindered and in perfect weather at 1406hrs Wg Cdr MacDougall

On the 24 July attack on Brest Wg Cdr MacDougall flew Fortress I AN530/WP-F. (90 Squadron Records)

Above: Sqn Ldr McLaren and crew in their thick flying clothing put on their parachutes before setting off for Brest on 24 July. (90 Squadron Records)

Below: Flt Lt Mathieson and crew before climbing into Fortress I AN529/WP-C and taking off for Brest on 24 July. (90 Squadron Records)

and Sqn Ldr McLaren opened the attack from 30,000ft. Two thousand feet above them was Flt Lt Mathieson. However, despite the claims made for the accuracy of the Sperry bombsight the bombs just missed *Gneisenau* and fell on the torpedo storage station on the west side of the Rade Abri quay and the outer corner of the dry dock. Two Bf 109s were seen trying to reach the Fortresses but then diverted away as the Hampdens began their attack. The Fortresses flew away unhindered and had all landed by 1545hrs. Unfortunately, the CO suffered from the high-altitude flying and was replaced three days later by Wg Cdr P. F. 'Tom' Webster.

Uneventful attacks on Hamburg and Kiel followed and then on 6 August Brest was again the target, though it was by now clear that the Fortress I had significant faults as an operational day bomber, not least its inadequate handheld defensive armament. The now promoted Sqn Ldr Mathieson flying AN529/WP-C and Plt Off Frank Sturmey's crew in AN523/WP-D left Polebrook at 0640hrs and flew uneventfully to Brest. Flying overhead at 32,000ft Plt Off Sturmey successfully bombed the dockyard and saw explosions on the shoreline and the Rade Abri. However, running in at 33,000ft it was discovered the bombsight in AN529 had iced over so Mathieson had to jettison the bomb load over the docks. Both then returned safely though somewhat worryingly, Mathieson's gunners reported that their gun mounts had frozen.

Sqn Ldr McLaren lifts Fortress I AN523/WP-D off from Polebrook en route to Brest on 24 July. (90 Squadron Records)

Ten days later at just after 0900hrs Plt Off Michael Wayman in AN532/WP-J and Plt Off Sturmey flying AN523/WP-D took off and again headed to Brest. Wayman's crew successfully bombed from 35,000ft, though cloud prevented the crew seeing any results and it returned safely to Polebrook landing at 1255hrs. Plt Off Frank Sturmey also bombed uneventfully from 32,000 feet at 1106hrs. However, three minutes later Flt Sgt Fred Goldsmith, the fire controller, spotted three Bf 109s of 1 and 3./JG 2 (which he identified as 'He 113s') with yellow noses approaching. The Fortress was attacked by at least five Bf 109s that over the next 23 minutes made 26 attacks which killed 19-year-old Flt Sgt Michael Leahy in the ventral gun position and 21-year-old Flt Sgt Sydney Ambrose in the beam. Another gunner, Sgt Harold Needle was badly wounded and Fred Goldsmith wounded in the hand and leg. The port outer engine had also been shattered.

The wireless operator urgently transmitted an SOS message as Frank Sturmey desperately dived the Fortress, though the 109s followed. Goldsmith continued to pass evasion calls as Sturmey manoeuvred the crippled aircraft as best he could whilst flying on three engines. Only when well over the Channel and 30 miles short of the English coast did the Messerschmitts withdraw. StabFw Erwin Kley of 3./JG 2 was later credited by the Luftwaffe with the destruction of the Fortress.

Sturmey headed the crippled Fortress for the nearest airfield at Roborough near Plymouth, and the aircraft crossed the coast at 600 feet. Despite having little rudder control and a shattered aileron Sturmey and his co-pilot Plt Off T. Franks managed to land safely though the large Fortress overran the short runway and struck a concrete tank trap. The wounded Sgt Needle was pulled clear, though he later died and within moments the aircraft burst into flames. This was the first Fortress to be lost to enemy action. For his coolness throughout, Flt Sgt Fred Goldsmith received the DFM.

It was the last Fortress I attack on the German capital ships in Brest.

# FLEDGED EAGLE
## 27 August 1941

When volunteer American pilots began arriving in Britain in the early part of WW2, they were readily accepted into the RAF that needed every pilot it could get. Initially they served with RAF units, often posing as Canadians, but as more volunteers arrived it was decided to group them in a special 'American' squadron – along the lines of the famous French Lafayette Escadrille of WW1. Thus 71 Squadron was formed, and became known as the Eagle Squadron after the national emblem of the United States.

One such volunteer was 24-year-old Plt Off W. R. 'Bill' Dunn from Minneapolis, Minnesota who after training joined the Eagle Squadron in April 1941. At that time 71 Squadron commanded by Sqn Ldr W. E. G. 'Bill' Taylor was flying Hurricane IIbs from Martlesham Heath, Suffolk and was engaged on cross-Channel sweeps. On 7 June Sqn Ldr Paddy Woodhouse took over and at the end of the month he led the squadron to North Weald, Essex from where operations would intensify. On a sweep near Lille at lunchtime on 2 July the Eagles saw their first action during a violent combat which resulted in claims for three Bf 109s destroyed. Flying Z3781/XR-A west of the town at 1235hrs Bill Dunn shot down one of the Messerschmitts to claim the first by an Eagle Squadron pilot. It was a big day for the American squadron.

Hurricane Mk.IIb Z3781/XR-A was regularly flown in by Bill Dunn and in which he achieved two of his victories. (W. R. Dunn via F. Olynyk)

Plt Off Bill Dunn in the cockpit of his Spitfire Mk. IIa of the Eagle Squadron during conversion training in August 1941. (W. R. Dunn via F. Olynyk)

To the west of Merville four days later Bill Dunn was escorting bombers on a 'Circus' against Lille when he shared the probable destruction of another with Plt Off Leon Jaugsch of 306 (Polish) Squadron. West of Lille on 21 July, and once more flying Z3781/XR-A, he shot down another Bf 109F for his second confirmed success. Dunn followed this up by shooting down another Bf 109F west of Mardyck at 1130hrs on 9 August to claim his final success with the Hurricane.

Just over a week later 71 Squadron's hopes were fulfilled when it was re-equipped with Spitfires, initially the Mk IIa. Bill Dunn was delighted, recalling: "The Spitfire was the absolute best. It is the only aircraft I've ever flown that had absolutely no bad habits."

The Eagle Squadron's first Spitfire operation was another Circus to the steel works at Lille on 27 August. The nine Blenheim bombers were escorted by 100 fighters, one of which was Spitfire IIa P7308/XR-D flown by Plt Off Dunn. As intended, the Luftwaffe was tempted up to battle and a vicious dogfight soon ensued over Ambleteuse at 0820hrs. Plt Off Bill Dunn described the engagement:

"I dived on one of two Me 109Fs, fired from 150 yards, and fired again. Pieces of the aircraft flew off and engine oil spattered my windscreen. The Me looked like a blowtorch as it went down. Tracers from another 109F behind me flashed past. I pulled back the throttle and skidded my plane sharply. The German overshot me by about ten feet, and I could see a red rooster painted on the side of the cockpit. The 109 was now within my range and with a burst of only three seconds I had him. A wisp of smoke turned almost instantly to flame. As it started down the tail broke off. I had my second victim of the day."

The Messerschmitt he so vividly described as carrying the red *Höllenhund* (Hound of Hell) was from 9./JG 26, but moments later as he fired on a third Messerschmitt, a burst of fire hit the cockpit of Dunn's Spitfire:

The red *Höllenhund* badge of 9./JG 26 carried on the Bf 109 engaged by Bill Dunn. (via C. H. Goss)

"Just as I started to press the gun button again my plane lurched sharply. I heard explosions. A ball of fire streamed through the cockpit, smashing into the instrument panel. There were two heavy blows against my right leg, and as my head snapped forward, I began to lose consciousness."

The German cannon shell had turned his right leg into a bloodied mess. He spun away, barely conscious:

"My mind cleared again and I realised that the earth was spinning up towards me. I tugged back on the control column and pulled into a gradual dive towards the English Channel. I checked the plane for damage. The tip of the right wing was gone. The rudder had been badly damaged. The instruments on the right side of the panel were shattered. There was blood on the cockpit floor. When I looked at my right leg I saw that the toe of the boot had been shot off. I could feel warm sticky fluid seeping from under my helmet to my neck and cheek. I gulped oxygen to fight off the nausea. I started to climb out of the cockpit. For some reason, I paused. The engine was still running all right and the plane seemed to be flyable. I slid back into my seat; I would try to make it home."

Escorted by two other Spitfires, Bill Dunn successfully landed at Hawkinge where he was gently lifted out and rushed off to hospital with much of his right foot missing. The severe injuries ended his career as an Eagle but in his last combat he had achieved the distinction of becoming the first American to achieve five victories in WW2.

The Eagles were now fully fledged.

Plt Off Bill Dunn's Spitfire IIA P7308/XR-D after he had landed it at Hawkinge on August 27, 1941 following his final combat with the damage readily visible on the rear fuselage. (RAF Hawkinge)

# A SLUGGING MATCH
# 21 November 1941

The South African Air Force provided a major part of the Allied fighter strength during the desert fighting in North Africa. One of its most notable units was 2 Squadron which, later nicknamed 'The Flying Cheetahs', had returned to action in October 1941 after a rest period. One newly arrived pilot was 2/Lt Eric Saville, always known as 'Danny', who had joined 2 Squadron on 15 October. Still four months short of his 20th birthday, he was soon in action.

Operation Crusader, the biggest Commonwealth offensive thus far in the desert, began on 18 November 1941. With heavy air support this resulted in some ferocious air fighting during the succeeding days.

At 1540hrs on the afternoon of Friday, 21 November, ten Curtiss Tomahawks of 4 Squadron SAAF, with a dozen more from 2 Squadron led by Maj Geoff Krummeck providing top cover, departed El Adem for a ground strafe on enemy armour that was retreating to the west of Tobruk. Shortly after the formation had crossed the line, they encountered black cloud at 2,500 feet and generally poor visibility which meant that the strafe was abandoned. However, despite the cloud hanging low over the desert,

Taken on 21 November 1941 Lt Danny Saville's Tomahawk, AK401/TA-C at El Adem after his encounter with the Italian MC.200 fighter showing the damage to it starboard wing resulting from a mid-air collision. (Gp Capt J. E. Pelly-Fry)

three Regia Aeronautica Italiana Macchi MC.200 Saetta fighters of the 373ª Squadriglia led by the CO Capitano Piero Raimondi were sighted flying on a similar course to the South Africans.

Lt 'Klippie' Stone pulled to the left and quickly broke up the enemy formation with one of the Saettas soon falling to his guns. At the controls of Tomahawk IIB AK401/TA-C Danny Saville pursued another and after a vigorous chase was soon involved in a tight turning fight with what was clearly an able pilot. The young South African manoeuvred so closely to the nimble Italian fighter that as he broke off his attack, his Tomahawk's starboard wing struck the Macchi violently very close to the cockpit. The Italian aircraft, thought to have been that flown by Cap Raimondi fell away whilst the impact spun Saville's Tomahawk through 90 degrees.

Cap Piero Raimondi the CO of the 373ª Squadriglia whose Macchi 200 collided with Saville's Tomahawk. (G. Massimello)

The Macchi's fate was not confirmed but some thought they saw it crash. Unfortunately all the records of the Italian unit were lost during the subsequent fighting. However, in his private daily diary Ten Gino Del Bufalo, a pilot of the same squadriglia, wrote:

"On November 21, late afternoon, my commander, Cap Piero Raimondi took off with two NCOs as wingmen but failed to return. Once back, the two related that they met at relatively low altitude 18 Hurricanes and a confused combat followed. One of them saw a Hurricane with a bent wing diving in front of him (no fire, no smoke) and at the same time Raimondi disappeared. No 'chute was seen."

No other Italian casualties were recorded on that day, so it is therefore likely that the collision with Saville's Tomahawk was the cause of Raimondi's loss. HQ 258 Wing credited the young South African with a probable for his first air combat claim, albeit achieved in somewhat unconventional circumstances. In the event, Piero Raimondi did manage to bale out and became a prisoner of war.

With several feet of his starboard wingtip bent downwards at right angles, it was only by some very skilful flying that Saville managed to land at El Adem.

The fight was by no means one sided, as elsewhere in the melee, 2/Lt Desmond Hinde had been hit and was last seen eight miles south of Gasr el Arid with the engine of his Tomahawk trailing thick black smoke. Finding he was too low to bale out Hinde crash-landed his blazing aircraft but he was safely picked up by armoured cars from 3 South African Armoured Car Regiment and eventually re-joined the squadron. The surviving Tomahawks landed back at El Adem at 1720hrs.

The following day in front of his battered aircraft, the youthful Saville was interviewed by the prominent American journalist Quentin Reynolds during which the South African commented that "… he had a bit of a slugging match with the Italian!"

Danny Saville's reputation as a skilled and aggressive pilot grew as his victories mounted during the fighting over the desert. He was rapidly promoted and eventually given command of 260 Squadron (RAF). Sadly, he was killed in action over Italy in September 1943. By this time he had been promoted to major and been awarded the DFC and bar and the US DFC and had still only reached the age of 21.

Lt Danny Saville looks ruefully at the bent wingtip of his Tomahawk during his interview with war correspondent Quentin Reynolds on 22 November. (SAAF)

# OUTNUMBERED OVER RANGOON
# 29 January 1942

Sent to reinforce the RAF in Burma 135 Squadron was commanded by of one of the RAF's leading fighter pilots, Sqn Ldr Frank Carey and by late January 1942 was established at Mingaladon for the defence of Rangoon. The squadron was equipped with Hurricane IIbs that had been hastily ferried out to Burma. Amongst its pilots was a 27-year-old Australian former school teacher, Plt Off Jack Storey who during a scramble against an inbound Japanese raid on 29 January achieved his first victory:

"I saw three enemy aircraft behind one P-40 which was easily being out-turned. We came down in a steep right-hand spiral at 310 this time and selected one enemy aircraft each. I got two steady bursts into mine, hits were observed and it slipped off into the

Jack Storey's first victim was this Nakajima Ki-27 of the 77th Sentai which in its death dive tried to crash into a parked Blenheim at Mingaladon. (W. J. Storey)

cloud to the left. Our ground crews saw an enemy fighter dive out of the cloud and crash near a Blenheim."

The Japanese were regularly targeting Rangoon and just before 0900hrs on Friday 6 February a raid was detected inbound to Mingaladon and P-40B Tomahawks of the American Volunteer Group (AVG) together with Hurricanes of 135 Squadron scrambled to intercept. With Sqn Ldr Carey's Hurricane becoming unserviceable on the ground leadership of the six Hurricanes was devolved to Plt Off Storey who was flying Z5659/WK-C. The fighters climbed rapidly into the sun with ground control stating the enemy were very high and in great numbers, but gave no directions. During the climb, two of the Hurricanes lost formation and passing 16,000ft Storey sighted the enemy about six miles off to his left and 5,000ft above. The enemy formation was a sweep by 25 highly manoeuvrable Nakajima Ki-27 'Nate' fighters of the veteran JAAF 50th and 77th Sentais.

Turning his four fighters to the right so as to get up sun, Jack Storey sighted three of the enemy fighters slightly above as they attempted to bounce the Hurricanes. He immediately entered a left-hand vertical spiral turn and when up sun fired a burst into one of the Nates. A whirling free-for-all fight then ensued with the Australian gaining a good position astern of another of the Japanese fighters and with a devastating burst of fire sent it spiralling to its destruction south of Zayatakwin. As the AVG P-40s arrived, Storey was being engaged from astern by two more Ki-27s. To evade their attack he spiralled left and rammed his throttle open, before once more climbing up sun before swooping on them. He made a quarter attack on the rearmost Ki-27

A pair of Hurricane IIbs of 135 Squadron are refuelled at Mingaladon in early February 1942. On the right is Z5659/WK-C which was flown by Plt Off Jack Storey in his combat on 6 February. He also flew it on the 23rd when he destroyed a Nate for his fourth victory. (W. J. Storey)

Plt Off Jack Storey was one of the most successful pilots of the first Burma campaign who claimed his first victory on his first operational sortie. (W. J. Storey)

firing two accurate bursts after which it spun to the right and crashed. He was again engaged by further Japanese fighters but evaded them, though his aircraft's Merlin engine was overheating. Despite this impediment, Jack Storey fired on two more Nates which he believed he probably hit, though did not observe the results. With his ammunition now gone, Storey managed to disengage and recover safely to Mingaladon where just one bullet hole was discovered in his wing – though all the plugs of his engine required changing.

In this epic fight against the odds, Plt Off Storey was credited with two Ki-27s destroyed and two probables from the total RAF claims for the engagement of three confirmed, three probables and three damaged. It is likely that one of Storey's victims was Lt Kitamura of the 77th Sentai.

On 23 February Jack Storey shot down his fourth Ki-27 which was his final claim of the campaign:

"I happened to notice out of the corner of my eye six fighters coming from my left. I set off after these. My man was a bit of a pushover for he was out to the right of the formation, curving round slowly, away from me, looking to see where the recce aircraft had got to and I got him very smartly. I got in an astern attack – I don't think he even saw me – and he was set on fire, crashed and burned in the trees from about 50 feet."

# SHREDDED!
## 12 February 1942

The air bombardment of Malta by the Luftwaffe and Regia Aeronautica was conducted to neutralise the potential for air and naval units based there to interdict the vital Axis air and sea supply route across the Mediterranean to North Africa. The 'eyes' for the naval and air strike forces was mainly from air reconnaissance that was largely provided by Luqa-based 69 Squadron. The squadron was equipped with Marylands that were supplemented with a few camera-equipped Hurricanes and Spitfires. However, from late 1941 losses had begun to rise alarmingly, in part due to the arrival in Sicily of Luftwaffe Messerschmitt Bf 109s that conducted an aggressive campaign over the island. In early January 1942 69 Squadron had 14 Marylands on strength, though the heavy blitz late in the month significantly reduced this number with many destroyed on the ground, including four on the 23rd and 24th alone. By the end of the month the squadron had just four serviceable aircraft, six more were unserviceable and four were awaiting formal write-off. One of the available Marylands was AR633 that had just returned to service following a wheels-up landing the previous November.

Fg Off Terry Channon who managed to successfully land his badly damaged Maryland. (via B. Cull)

During the afternoon of 12 February Plt Off Terry Channon left Luqa in Maryland I AR733 with his crew of Plt Off Cliff Beer as observer and wireless operator/air gunners Sgts Arthur Moore and Bob Watson. They conducted a shipping search patrol between the island of Pantelleria and Cap Bon on the Tunisian coast and on completion of their task they set course

Ltn Herbert Schramm of 8./JG 53 who had misidentified the Maryland as a Blenheim. (via C. H. Goss)

back to Malta. At 1820hrs when approximately eight miles south of the island the Maryland was intercepted by a pair of Messerschmitt Bf 109F-4/trops of 8./JG 53 based at Comiso, in southern Sicily. Led by Ltn Herbert Schramm, the two fighters rapidly closed on the Maryland and on their first pass opened fire from just 40 yards. It was a devastating burst that killed the unfortunate Moore in the top turret, caused severe damage to the fuselage and tail and started several fires, including a serious one in the bomb-bay fuel tank.

Despite being wounded in four places, Watson disregarded his injuries and painfully crawled into the rear of the aircraft which was by now filled with smoke and flame, though this eased as the blazing bomb-bay tank fell away just before reaching the coast. Dragging the body of his comrade out of the turret Bob Watson then manned it himself as the two Messerschmitts closed for a second pass. When the fighters came within range Watson opened fire with an accurate burst into the second fighter as it flew by and, obviously hit, it appeared to fall away into the sea in flames. There was, however, no corresponding German loss though what they saw was possibly the blazing fuel tank hitting the sea. Fortunately, the other fighter then disengaged and flew off. As Terry Channon steered the shattered Maryland towards base the gallant Watson once again attempted to quell the blaze by throwing out burning equipment.

The shattered wreck of Maryland I AR733 on Luqa airfield following its crash landing. The smoke-blackened holes in the mid fuselage are mute testimony to Sgt Watson's bravery. (A. F. Chivers)

He also beat out the flames on the clothing of Moore's body in the process of which he sustained severe burns himself.

Though barely conscious Watson then assisted Terry Channon as he brought the shattered and still burning Maryland into an excellent belly landing at Luqa, that with no flaps meant touching down at 140mph. As emergency crews surrounded the aircraft, Sgt Bob Watson was rushed off for emergency treatment for his injuries. Afterwards, the ground crew counted over 60 cannon and machine-gun holes in the wrecked aircraft. It never flew again and those who saw the battered Maryland were astonished that it had actually stayed in the air.

As for the Germans, on return to Sicily, Herbert Schramm was credited with a Blenheim destroyed that was his 38th confirmed victory – and the Staffel's 605th. Shortly afterwards Schramm returned to Germany for instructional duties until mid-1943. He was then given command of 5./JG 27 on home-defence duties but was shot down and killed by USAAF fighters on 1 December. For his selfless courage and resilience, Sgt Bob Watson received an immediate award of the DFM while Channon continued flying with 69 Squadron and later received a DSO.

This close-up of the tail of the Maryland shows the damage inflicted by the Messerschmitts' cannon fire. (A. F. Chivers)

# SMOKING OVER DIEPPE
# 19 August 1942

On the morning of 19 August 1942 the Allies launched a large-scale raid on the enemy-held port of Dieppe on the northern coast of France. Operation Jubilee involved the landing of almost 10,000 men from a large landing fleet under massive air cover which resulted in some of the heaviest air fighting of the war to that point. The Blenheims of 13 Squadron were tasked to effectively screen anti-aircraft batteries that commanded the cliffs on the left-hand side of Dieppe town by dropping phosphorous smoke bombs. These were described as 'large biscuit tins filled with a compound that ignited and made masses of smoke when exposed to air'.

Their target was the Bismarck battery on the cliffs to the north of the town

The two morning 13 Squadron 'vics' were led by Flt Lts Eric Beverley (left) and John Shaw.
(E. Beverley via N. L. R. Franks)

above 'Blue' beach. Commanded by Wg Cdr W. J. Tailyour and usually based at Odiham, the squadron had been detached for the operation to Thruxton, Hampshire and the previous evening crews were briefed on their operational task. It was therefore still dark when the crews woke. The Blenheims would be the first RAF aircraft over Dieppe as their smoke screens were seen as essential to shield the landing craft as they approached the beaches. The first 'vic' of three was led by Flt Lt Eric Beverley who eased the heavily laden Z6089/OO-F off from Thruxton at 0410hrs with Plt Off Dave Rogan in Z5811/OO-P, closely followed a few minutes later by Plt Off Cecil

Woodland's crew in V5380. The formation was quickly followed by a further 'vic' led by Flt Lt John Shaw in Z5882 leading Z6558 with Plt Off Beck and Plt Off Alaric Jickling flying N3545/OO-K.

Each aircraft carried a full load of the 100lb phosphorous bombs in canisters that required the removal of the bomb doors. The six Blenheims flew into the lightening sky in the dawn twilight. Sunrise was at 0550hrs though the first landing craft were scheduled to be approaching the beaches at around 0445hrs. However, the Blenheim pilots had difficulty in joining up into formation in the dark. Nonetheless, each aircraft made successful drops of their smoke bombs with the resulting screen effectively blinding the two batteries.

Flt Lt Beverley recalled:

"We flew low to avoid the radar cover and our route took us just north of the ships of the attacking force. The white cliffs to the north of Dieppe stood out clearly in the morning light and we pulled up to our aiming point, a small bay to the south-west along the line of the cliff face where the gun emplacements were and went into line astern to lay our smoke as low as we could fly. There was little or no AA fire until we had finished our smoke laying but then we were over the port itself and there we encountered a considerable amount of flak. We then turned seaward and had to pass low over the attacking fleet. They were understandably somewhat trigger happy and the silhouette of a Blenheim not being noticeably different from a Ju 88 they let us have it just in case.

"Either as a result of the anti-aircraft fire from Dieppe or from the Royal Navy, I suffered damage to my port engine and flying controls and lost all my hydraulics. I could not operate my flaps or wheels and had to make a belly landing."

Flt Lt Eric Beverley's Blenheim comes to a halt following its wheels-up landing after it had sustained damage over Dieppe. (13 Squadron Records)

Plt Off Alaric Jickling leaps from his Blenheim at Thruxton after returning safely from the morning sortie to Dieppe.
(13 Squadron Records)

After being airborne for 2½ hours, five of 13 Squadron's aircraft had returned to Thruxton by 0640hrs with Beverley's skidding to a halt without its undercarriage whilst the others landed safely. However, Cecil Woodland's aircraft was missing, thought to have been hit by enemy fire from a coastal battery and to have crashed. He with Sgts Henry Neville and Austin Boyd were the RAF's first casualties of Operation Jubilee.

The smoke-laying plan required further sorties later in the morning to cover the withdrawal phase and a further mission was prepared. At 1100hrs Flt Lt Thomas eased Z6358/OO-M off Thruxton's grass runway leading Plt Offs Broughton (Z5882) and Kilpatrick (N3612) and followed the Blenheims of 614 Squadron out across the Channel towards Dieppe. Navigation was easy as large palls of smoke hung over the port. However, when halfway across the Channel, the fighter escort for 13 Squadron's 'vic' indicated they were returning to base. With the skies above Dieppe a veritable hornet's nest of enemy fighters, Thomas had no option but to turn around, thus bringing 13 Squadron's part in Operation Jubilee to a rather unsatisfactory end.

The abortive afternoon smoke-laying sortie to Dieppe was led by Flt Lt Thomas flying Blenheim IV Z6358/OO-M. (via R. C. B. Ashworth)

# ALEUTIAN DOGFIGHT
# 25 September 1942

After the outbreak of war in the Pacific, the Kittyhawks of 111 (F) Squadron RCAF under Sqn Ldr Deane Nesbitt were moved to Patricia Bay on Canada's Pacific coast. Then, following the Japanese landings on the Aleutian Islands, in June 1942 it was one of several Canadian squadrons deployed for service in Alaska. The squadron moved with its Kittyhawk Is to Elmendorf near Anchorage where it provided the air defence for the area against the perceived threat from marauding Japanese carriers. On 17 August 111 Squadron came under command of Sqn Ldr Ken Boomer who the previous year had flown Spitfires in the UK. He soon joined a detachment forward at Umnak Island for operations against the Japanese that were established in the western Aleutians on the islands of Attu and Kiska. At Umnak the 111 Squadron detachment flew USAAF P-40K Warhawks that retained their US serial numbers though they had RCAF markings overpainted on the USAAF stars and, initially at least, the unit's 'LZ' code letters.

Soon afterwards the newly developed airfield at Adak put the enemy bases just within range of the P-40s and so when the Canadians arrived Boomer was soon chafing to get his men onto an offensive mission. He was given his wish and the Canadians were

included in the escort for an attack on Kiska planned for 25 September. The nine B-24 Liberators for the attack were given a heavy fighter escort of a dozen P-39 Airacobras and 20 P-40s. Four of the P-40s were flown by Canadians

Sqn Ldr Ken Boomer who achieved the only RCAF victory over North America during WW2. (RCAF)

Plt Off Hal Gooding (left) and Fg Off Jim Gohl participated in the attack on Kiska on 25 September. (RCAF)

with Sqn Ldr Boomer joined by Fg Off Jim Gohl, Fg Off Rob Lynch and Plt Off Hal Gooding. This was the RCAF's first offensive mission of the Aleutians campaign.

After the lengthy overwater flight the B-24s completed their bombing runs and the fighters then dived down and strafed gun emplacements and naval craft in the harbour. However, to oppose the attack two Nakajima A6M2-N 'Rufe' floatplanes of the Imperial Japanese Navy's 5th Kokutai flown by Lt Yamada and his (unidentified) wingman had taken off from the harbour. The Canadian quartet flew in low towards the north head of Kiska harbour where they struck at gun positions as well as the main Japanese camp and a radar installation.

Nakajima A6M-2 'Rufe' floatplane fighters of the 5th Kokutai anchored at Kiska, two of which were shot down during the 25 September attack. (US Navy)

As they swung round for a second pass they met the two floatplanes, one (believed to have been that flown by Yamada) quickly getting onto the tail of a P-40 from the US 11th Fighter Squadron. The Rufe was attacked in turn by Sqn Ldr Boomer who pulled up and opened fire as he later recalled: "I climbed to a stall practically, pulled right up under him. I just poured it into him from underneath. He flamed up and went down and the Japanese pilot jumped just before it hit the sea." Very soon afterwards Maj John Chenault CO of the 11th FS shot down the second Rufe.

Parked at Adak before the Kiska mission is P-40K Warhawk 42-45945/LZ-F, of 111 Squadron RCAF that was flown by Sqn Ldr Ken Boomer. The 'LZ' code letters have been overpainted. (via L. Milberry)

The Canadian section then joined several US aircraft in strafing a surfaced Japanese submarine until their ammunition was expended. Ken Boomer again described the attack: "We poured so much 50 calibre stuff onto the decks that it glowed red hot and killed three gun crews. The boys just waited their turn and came down at it."

With few Japanese aircraft in the area, Sqn Ldr Boomer's victory was a rare event. Indeed his was to be the only 'kill' by the RCAF over North America and was in fact the only air combat for the 'home-based' RCAF. Ken Boomer was awarded an immediate DFC, the citation for which read:

"Inspired by his unflagging zeal and devotion to duty his squadron has maintained a consistently high standard of efficiency under difficult and trying conditions. He has displayed great qualities of courage and determination in seeking out the enemy and his flying skill has been responsible for the excellent work done by his squadron in action against the enemy."

All four Canadian pilots were also awarded the US Air Medal.

The Canadians did not participate in any further offensive operations during 1942 and in mid-October 111 (F) Squadron moved back to Kodiak for defensive duties.

# A BAD DAY AT THE OFFICE
# 29 September 1942

Early on the afternoon of 29 September 1942 a Luftwaffe Junkers Ju 52 transport set off on a routine flight over the Western Desert but had the misfortune to encounter a trio of Spitfires, a type only recently introduced to service there. For the unfortunate Ju 52 crew it really was not their day as all three of the pilots were experienced and successful.

Flying Spitfire Vc BP798/ZX-X, the formation was led by 23-year-old Sqn Ldr Pete Matthews, a veteran of the Battle of France and the Battle of Britain, who had taken command of 145 Squadron at the end of August. On 11 September, just a couple of days before taking over, during a combat west of El Alamein he shot down a Bf 109F and so achieved 'ace' status and ended the war with a total of nine victories. His No. 2 was 27-year-old Flt Lt John 'Crash' Curry from Dallas, Texas. He was an experienced barnstorming pilot and when WW2 broke out he promptly joined the RCAF, arriving in England in 1941. He later joined 601 Squadron flying a Spitfire from the deck of the aircraft carrier HMS *Eagle* to reinforce Malta where he soon claimed his first victory. When the squadron moved to Egypt he became a flight commander and began scoring regularly and by 29 September had taken his personal 'score' to four confirmed victories. His fourth victory on 7 September

Plt Off Ray Sherk in the cockpit of his Spitfire before moving to Egypt. (R. Sherk)

Flying Spitfire Vc BR392/UF-P Flt Sgt Ray Sherk opened the attack on Horst Willborn's Ju 52, his cannon fire setting the transport on fire before the other two delivered the *coup de grâce*. (R. Sherk)

may have been a significant scalp as it was thought to be the Messerschmitt 109 flown by Ltn Hans-Arnold Stahlschmidt of I./JG 27, a holder of the Knight's Cross who had 59 victories. He was flying Spitfire BR469/UF-B when he encountered the Ju 52.

The final member of the triumvirate was 20-year-old Canadian Plt Off Ray Sherk who after training had arrived in England and had a successful tour in 129 Squadron flying sweeps from Westhampnett during which he shot down two German fighters.

Ltn Horst Willborn who survived the attack and crash landing on 29 September. (H. Willborn)

Junkers Ju 52 W/nr 5480/'NQ+AV' of 10 (Flg) Kp Ln Rgt 40 burns in the desert after being shot down by the Spitfires near Charing Cross. (H. Willborn)

He had then been commissioned and posted to the Middle East where he joined 601 Squadron. On the 29th he was at the controls of Spitfire Vc BR392/UF-P for his encounter with the German trimotor transport.

The three Spitfires lifted off from the patch of desert optimistically named 'Landing Ground 92' at 1340hrs to attack a train reported on the railway to the west of Mersa Matruh. They did not find the train but near to 'Charing Cross' spotted Junkers Ju 52 W/nr 5480/'NQ+AV' of 10 (Flg)Kp Ln Rgt 40 flying westwards at just 200 feet. Ray Sherk opened the attack as the Junkers pilot desperately attempted to land on the desert. He was followed first by Pete Matthews then 'Crash' Curry also attacked. In its desperate evasion the port wing of the transport struck the ground and it crashed. Matthews then attacked again causing it to burst into flames. It had been the misfortune of the Ju 52 crew not only to encounter three of the RAF's best fighters in the desert, but also flown by three of its more accomplished pilots.

Unfortunately for Ray Sherk having opened fire to begin the demise of the Junkers transport on the way home his Spitfire ran out of fuel and he had to force land on the eastern end of the Qattara Depression and was later captured.

It really had been a bad day at the office – not only for the Germans but also for one of their conquerors.

# SIX BOTTLES OF BEER!
# 26 December 1942

To support the Australian Army in the capture of Buna on the north coast of New Guinea, Gen Blamey, the Australian commander, requested an army co-operation squadron operating 'a relatively slow aircraft'. Thus, in November 1942 4 Squadron RAAF flying the two-seat CAC Wirraway under Wg Cdr Dallas Charlton was deployed from Australia to 12-Mile Strip (Berry) at Port Moresby. It was trained for, among other roles, artillery spotting, a key task in the jungle warfare that confronted the Australian troops.

On 26 November 4 Squadron sent two detached flights from Port Moresby north of the Owen Stanley mountains, one to Dobodura to co-operate with 2/5th Field Regiment supporting 'Bullforce' and the other to Popondetta, about six miles south of Gona to work with 'Blackforce'. Sortie briefings were conducted at Dobodura by Capt R. J. C. O'Loan, the army liaison officer who was in regular radio contact with the artillery units. After one of the first spotting sorties, the squadron received a congratulatory signal from New Guinea Force HQ for the excellence of the spotting that had allowed a 25pdr battery to destroy three Japanese anti-aircraft guns at Buna.

Two Wirraways after landing at Popondetta on 26 December with A20-103 on the left shortly after Plt Off Archer had leaped out to run to the control tent to announce his success. (RAAF Museum, Point Cook)

Both Fg Off Archer and his gunner Sgt Les Coulston were decorated for their actions on 26 December 1942. (RAAF Museum, Point Cook)

The Wirraway crews also flew some photographic sorties. As well as their spotting tasks, eager for any offensive work, on 7 December the 4 Squadron crews also began some fighter-bomber action when eight Wirraways attacked Japanese troop positions near Gona mission with 250lb bombs. To evade the anticipated anti-aircraft fire the attack was made from very low level that also offered an element of protection from marauding Japanese fighters. However, during mid-December the squadron suffered the loss of two Wirraways to weather over the Owen Stanley mountains and another shot down during a survey flight over the battle area.

The first month of operations for 4 Squadron was to end with a remarkable incident on 26 December. That morning Fg Off Jack Archer and Sgt Les Coulston took off in Wirraway A20-103/D to fly a recce of the wrecked Japanese ship *Ayatosan Maru* grounded offshore from Gona. Flying over the target at 1145hrs Archer spotted a Japanese fighter that the crew identified as a 'Zero' about 1,000ft below them. Acting on impulse, without hesitation and despite the manifest difference in performance, using his height advantage, Archer pushed the Wirraway into a dive onto the fighter and fired a five-second burst using the two front-firing Browning .303in machine guns. As he pulled away to continue his recce task Archer saw the Japanese fighter crash into the sea about 100 yards offshore.

After completing their recce task Archer returned to Popondetta and barely had the Wirraway come to a stop than he leaped from the aircraft and ran to the control tent.

On entering he shouted: "Sir, sir, I think I've shot down a Zero!" He was told in no uncertain terms that Wirraways could not shoot down Zeros but Archer then outlined the event: "I went in to look at the wreck off Gona and I saw this thing in front of me and it had red spots on it, so I gave it a burst and it appeared to fall into the sea." Within minutes the incredulous operations officer had received calls or messages from 2/14th and 2/16th Battalion's observers around the Gona area confirming the story.

Shortly afterwards at the 4 Squadron HQ, Wg Cdr Charlton received an understandably elated message from the detachment that read: "Archer has shot down one Zeke, repeat one Zeke. Send six bottles of beer." In an area where beer was likened to liquid gold, this was indeed a reward and the precious commodity was duly despatched for Archer and Coulston to celebrate their unique victory.

This was the only occasion in which a Wirraway crew was to shoot down a Japanese aircraft. However, in New Guinea, any Japanese fighter was generally described as a 'Zero' but the Mitsubishi A6M Zeros of the Imperial Japanese Navy had recently been reinforced by elements of the Japanese Army Air Force's 11th Sentai equipped with the Nakajima Ki-43 'Oscar'. This too was radial engined and it was in fact one of these of the 11th Sentai's 1st Chutai flown by W/O Tadashi Yoshitake that had been shot down. When his body was recovered, it was found that he had been hit in the head, and probably died instantaneously.

Ground crew were quick to adorn Jack Archer's Wirraway with a Japanese flag victory marking as LAC Joe Booker indicates. (RAAF Museum, Point Cook)

Brig Ennis C. Whitehead presents Fg Off Archer with the US Silver Star for combat valour – a rare award to a non-American. (RAAF Museum, Point Cook)

For this feat on 19 January 1943 Fg Off J. S. Archer was awarded the US Silver Star for combat valour by the Allied Supreme Commander of the Southwest Pacific Area, Gen Douglas MacArthur. The citation stated: "…doing the impossible – shooting down a Zero and bringing home his observer to tell the tale." The presentation was made by Brig Ennis C. Whitehead, the Commanding General Allied Air Forces in New Guinea whilst for his part Sgt J. L. Coulston was mentioned in despatches.

# A CLOSE SHAVE
# 3 March 1943

Flt Sgt Aubrey Hilliard of 235 Squadron who had a close shave with an Fw 190 off the coast of Norway. (A. H. Hilliard)

The Beaufighter-equipped 235 Squadron was based at RAF Leuchars on the Scottish east coast. It was one of Coastal Command's 'strike' squadrons tasked with the destruction of enemy coastal shipping in the sea lanes off Occupied Europe. These patrols over some inhospitable seas and along the rugged coastline of German-occupied Norway were no sinecure for crews with the hostile weather as much of a threat as the Luftwaffe. On 3 March 1943, the squadron was tasked with escorting six Hampden torpedo-bombers of 455 Squadron in a dusk sweep off the Norwegian coast. The seven Beaufighters of 235 Squadron led by Wg Cdr Baird in 'T' lifted off at 1600hrs and headed for the enemy coast in indifferent weather of low cloud and poor visibility; flying Beaufighter Ic T3295/A was Flt Sgt Aubrey Hilliard with his observer, Flt Sgt Jimmy Hoyle.

The fighter defence of southern Norway was the responsibility of I Gruppe, JG 5 (I./JG 5) flying the Focke-Wulf Fw 190A under Hptm Gerhardt von Wehren. Its three Staffeln were based around the coast and at Herdla was 1./JG 5 led by Obtl Gerd Senoner.

Flying at only 500 feet above the waves, the Beaufighters had to orbit in a wide circle astern of the slower Hampdens and as they neared the coast, a fighter was sighted. Aubrey Hilliard related the subsequent events:

"Our task on this particular day in March was to escort Hampden bombers to the Norwegian coast, arriving there about 30 minutes before dusk. On nearing the coast south of Stavanger as the rear aircraft, my observer called, 'Enemy aircraft at nine o'clock same level coming straight towards us'. I saw it, opened the throttles and turned towards him. He pulled hard and as it went past 200 yards to port, I recognised it as a Fw 190. The formation had turned south and was a long way off and the 190 continued to port to north-east as I levelled out south-west. At about 800 yards in my four o'clock he began firing, I noticed the usual one-in-three tracers as I pulled sharply to starboard in a steep turn towards him again and he pulled up and to starboard. It was happening so quickly as the 190 was so manoeuvrable and fast, my Beaufighter on the other hand was shuddering at 260 knots as I headed west carrying out 'corkscrew' action between 0 and 500 feet. Skipping the waves was hair raising, let alone being attacked by enemy aircraft and many times I was low enough for his tracer to go over me."

Aubrey Hilliard's Beaufighter wore the short-lived white fuselage with camouflaged top surfaces and was the only one on the squadron not fitted with a rear gun. He continued:

"Jimmy, my observer, gave me good positions of where the Fw 190 was, and he flashed his Aldis lamp at him to mimic gun flashes. A few more attacks took place and each time I took evasive action corkscrewing then turning towards the 190 to create turbulence for him and lessen his deflection. After each attack, I steep-turned west getting further away from the enemy coast. The combat lasted for about seven minutes. He had hit me several times, including the starboard engine and wing – I saw the tracer go in, but I was unable to make an attack on him – he was too manoeuvrable and fast, I was therefore out to save ourselves."

This Focke-Wulf Fw 190A 'White 6' of 1./JG 5 parked on the wooden-planked hardstanding at Herdla in the spring of 1943 is possibly the aircraft flown by Fw Josef Gruber. (via J. Weal)

The scars of the battle are readily seen on the battered Beaufighter Ic T3295/A at Arbroath the morning after their encounter off Norway. (A. H. Hilliard)

As the range from the coast increased the Focke-Wulf pilot decided to withdraw, leaving a relieved RAF crew to contemplate the long crossing of the North Sea in their damaged aircraft. Their assailant was almost certainly Fw Josef Gruber of 1./JG 5 flying Fw 190A-2 W/nr 2132 'White 6' who at 1832hrs (German time) was reported as encountering a number of enemy aircraft and without doubt was Aubrey Hilliard's persistent assailant though he failed to return, probably falling victim to the bad weather.

After the Fw 190 had pulled away it was soon lost in the murk as Hilliard gingerly eased the damaged Beaufighter up to about 7,000 feet continually monitoring the suspect starboard engine and flew back to Scotland with Hoyle navigating by dead reckoning as the W/T set had been destroyed. The crew made their landfall in the dark just south of Peterhead and after a time Hilliard spotted a set of runway lights and put down at 2035hrs. They had landed without brakes at HMS Condor, the Fleet Air Arm station at Arbroath and came to rest just in front of a massive post. The following morning Hilliard and Hoyle examined their stricken Beaufighter which with cannon holes in the fuselage, starboard engine and propeller had to be written off. The Luftwaffe pilot had, unknowingly, achieved his objective.

# A KIWI FIRST
# 6 May 1943

During the desperate fighting at Guadalcanal, in October 1942 the Americans requested an RNZAF fighter squadron be deployed to Tonga. No. 15 Squadron was selected taking over some well-worn USAAF P-40Ks that were used until moving forward to Espiritu Santo in the New Hebrides in March 1943. Sadly, Sqn Ldr Allan Crighton, the CO, was killed in an accident on the 25th so was replaced by Flt Lt Mike Herrick, who despite his combat experience was still only 21.

At Espiritu Santo, 15 Squadron was re-equipped with new Kittyhawk IIIs and on 26 April moved north to Kukum Field on Guadalcanal, described by the squadron diarist as 'a depressingly primitive spot'. By this time, the island had been fully secured, though remained subject to frequent Japanese air raids. The squadron flew its first shipping escort patrols on the 29th. Defensive patrols over Guadalcanal and the Russell Islands, where a US base had been secured were also flown.

Kittyhawk III NZ3075 '24' flown by Sqn Ldr Herrick leads Flt Lt Duncan in NZ3060 '9' seen from the Hudson they were escorting shortly before sighting the Japanese floatplane. (RNZAF)

The New Zealand fighters finally had their first contact with the Japanese on 6 May. That morning 15 Squadron was tasked to escort an RNZAF Hudson from 3 Squadron into 'the Slot' to an area off Simbo Island where enemy aircraft were known to be active. Flying Kittyhawk III NZ3075 '24' Sqn Ldr Mike Herrick and Flt Lt Sholto Duncan in NZ3060 '9' provided the escort. In poor weather as they approached the area the Hudson descended to 500ft with the two fighters positioned astern at 3,000ft. Looking out of the astrodome, one of the Hudson crew spotted a floatplane about three miles away at 1,500 feet though initially neither of the fighter pilots could see it. Therefore, the Hudson pilot set off in pursuit but then lost visual contact in a heavy rainstorm.

Eventually, the newly promoted Sqn Ldr Herrick saw the floatplane that was still about three miles away on the edge of a bank of heavy black cloud flying at about 800ft. The two Kittyhawks descended to just above the floatplane that they patiently stalked and eventually identified as a Nakajima E8N-1 'Dave'. As they closed in the two Kittyhawk pilots jettisoned their drop tanks and, having called "Tally-ho!", Herrick and Duncan quickly closed the distance on the unsuspecting Japanese floatplane. It made no attempt to seek the sanctuary of the adjacent cloud

The oil slick and wreckage photographed by the Hudson crew marking the demise of the E8N-1 'Dave' that was the first victory by RNZAF fighters in the Pacific. (RNZAF)

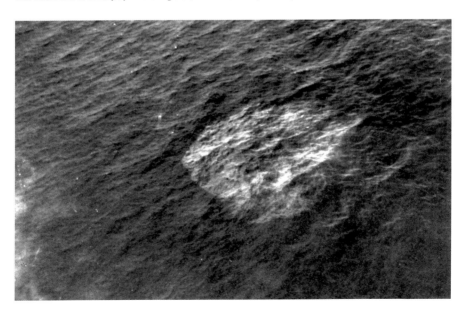

Sqn Ldr Mike Herrick in the cockpit of his Kittyhawk which displays the Japanese kill marking to add to his claims over German aircraft. (RNZAF)

as the fighters descended and closed from behind and slightly below. Having closed to about 200 yards directly astern Mike Herrick followed by Sholto Duncan each fired several bursts from 200 yards. The 'Dave' immediately burst into flames and went blazing into the sea leaving just a patch of oil and a wing floating on the surface.

The wreckage was photographed by the Hudson crew which provided evidence of 15 Squadron's first success that was credited shared by both pilots. This was also the first of the 99 victories that RNZAF fighters were credited with in the South Pacific. On returning to Guadalcanal his ground crew proudly painted a Japanese flag to join the crosses representing Herrick's claims against German aircraft flying with the RAF over England. Sqn Ldr Herrick went on to claim three more victories over the Solomon Islands while Flt Lt Duncan added a Zero to his score the following month.

During several tours 15 Squadron flew more sorties than any other New Zealand fighter squadron in the Pacific theatre and with 23 Japanese aircraft destroyed was the joint top-scoring RNZAF squadron.

# TIMOR ACE
# 9 October 1943

In July 1943 Sqn Ldr Reginald 'Butch' Gordon joined the Beaufighter-equipped 31 Squadron RAAF at Coomalie Creek near Darwin as a flight commander. The squadron was tasked with making sweeps north to the Japanese-occupied island of Timor that lasted up to six hours. On 11 August Gordon led nine Beaufighters to attack the seaplane base at Taberfane in the Aru Islands across the Arafura Sea. As the Beaufighters ran in they were engaged by three Nakajima A6M-2 'Rufe' and two Mitsubishi F1M2 'Pete' floatplanes, one of which was damaged by Gordon for his first air combat claim. Several more raids followed before on 9 October came an epic fight when Butch Gordon led an armed recce by six Beaufighters over Selaroe Island.

He was flying Beaufighter Ic A19-40/EH-G with his regular navigator, Flt Sgt Ron Jordan who spotted a twin-engined Kawasaki Ki-45 'Nick' heavy fighter over the target as Gordon recalled soon afterwards:

The only RAAF Beaufighter pilot to become an ace in the Pacific theatre was Sqn Ldr 'Butch' Gordon of 31 Squadron who had spent much of the early war years as an instructor. (K. MacDonald)

"The aircraft was intercepted by a twin-engined fighter coming from NW at 800 feet and 235 knots which fired from 300 yards, seven o'clock passing through to two o'clock. We turned toward E/A as it turned south, jettisoned bombs and followed, closing up to 25 yards and opened fire. E/A commenced to disintegrate and crash into the sea from a left-hand stall turn. It had taken slight evasive action to allow his rear gunner to fire, hitting the starboard mainplane and shooting the starboard engine exhaust ring off. The E/A was destroyed."

Gordon then continued strafing some ground targets but on returning over Selaroe Island was attacked by another 'Nick'. He reported afterwards:

Sqn Ldr Gordon's first two victims were Ki-45 'Nick' fighters shot down on 9 October 1943 off Selaroe Island. The demise of the second was caught on camera. (RAAF)

"Just on leaving the island saw an E/A flying south and 3 minutes later it attacked from seven o'clock, 200 yards away, closed to 100 yards and hit port engine and starboard aileron and passed across taking up position 400 yards to starboard then turned across to pursue the formation in front. I opened up both engines and fired from 350 yards and E/A commenced to burn from port wing root. Still burning it slowly lost height and crashed into the sea about 15 miles south of Selaroe Island."

Having claimed their first air combat victories for Butch Gordon and Ron Jordan the excitement was not yet over. During the long flight home over the shark-infested Timor Sea the Beaufighter suffered an engine failure but by skilful flying, Gordon reached land and was forced to make a crash landing at Livingstone, a few miles north of Coomalie. Soon afterwards his aggressive leadership was rewarded with a DFC.

The squadron next attacked Taberfane on 21 November, covering a B-25 raid but near the target two A6M-2N 'Rufe' floatplane fighters appeared. Gordon immediately attacked one head on:

"We made a 12 o'clock attack from above on a 'Rufe', which, when 100 yards away did a half roll on its back, and attempted to dive away below. I did an aileron turn in an attempt to follow it down. The 'Rufe' burst into flames and crashed 500 yards off shore."

Then on 16 December during a convoy attack off the Timor coast Butch Gordon and his No. 2, Flt Sgt Fergusson engaged four Ki-45 'Nicks' near Lautern. Gordon hit one in the wing roots from about 100 yards as it hung in a stall turn before falling into the sea and breaking up. He then turned and opening fire he damaged a second fighter.

The action over the Japanese-occupied islands of the Dutch East Indies continued into 1944 when on 4 January 31 Squadron Beaufighters led by Sqn Ldr Gordon

escorted a raid by Dutch-manned B-25s of 18 (NEI) Squadron. South of Cape Mali on the south-western point of Timor he spotted a Mitsubishi G4M 'Betty' twin-engine bomber which immediately dived to sea level. Gordon described how he became the only Beaufighter pilot to become an ace of the south-west Pacific theatre:

"When about 10 miles south of Cape Mali No. 2 reported an enemy aeroplane approaching from the two o'clock position. I called F/O Archer to join me and did a right-hand climbing turn and commenced a quarter astern lower attack, developing into a stern attack. After one long burst, I saw both engines catch fire. I then did an aileron turn and returned to my original position in the formation. The enemy aeroplane continued to burn and the starboard wing and other parts flew off before it went into the sea where it exploded. After the explosion, petrol burned on the water with smoke rising several hundred feet."

Soon afterwards 'Butch' Gordon received a bar to his DFC but on 27 February he flew an air test to check one of the propellers. Tragically during the test the 'good' engine's propeller feathered and the aircraft crashed killing the crew. It was a sad end to a very accomplished pilot.

# FATAL ENCOUNTER
# 16 February 1944

After a period in dock for repair, on 12 January 1944 the Avenger-class escort carrier HMS *Biter* re-embarked 811 Naval Air Squadron under Lt Cdr E. B. Morgan. The squadron was equipped for the trade protection role and in addition to its main equipment of Fairey Swordfish for anti-submarine work, also had a fighter flight that comprised a trio of Grumman Wildcats for air-defence tasks. After a brief work-up in early February *Biter* sailed as part of the escort for the slow convoy ONS29 bound for Halifax, Nova Scotia, before switching to cover the southbound convoy OS 68/KMS 42 heading for Gibraltar and Freetown, Sierra Leone. By the morning of 16 February *Biter* and the convoy were 'zigzagging' southwards some 170 miles to the west of Ireland when the ship's radar detected an unidentified contact approaching.

Based at Mont-de-Marsan in German-occupied south-west France under control of Fleigerführer Atlantik was Fernaufklärungsgruppe 5 (FAGr 5) that had arrived in France for operations in late 1943. Under the Gruppenkommandeur Hptm Herman Fischer the unit was equipped with large Junkers Ju 290As for long-range patrols over the Atlantic to locate convoys and report to waiting U-boat packs. The heavily armed four-engined aircraft were also equipped with Hs 293 glider bombs for shipping attack and were thus formidable opponents. In early February, the Gruppe had dispatched aircraft west of Biscay to locate convoys and to support attacks by submarines and missile-carrying aircraft and worked hard to maintain contact.

At 0500hrs on the morning of 16 February Ju 290A-5 W/nr 0175 '9V+FH' of 1./FAGr 5 flown by Ltn Eberhard Elfert lifted off from Mont-de-Marsan briefed to fly into the Atlantic to 14 degrees west to relocate and shadow the convoy OS 68/KMS 42. It was followed three hours later by Ju 290 W/nr 0177 '9V+DK' of 2./FAGr 5 with its 11-man crew led by Hptm Karl-Friedrich Bergen the Staffelkapitän. At 1040hrs Elfert's crew located the southbound ships of OS68 but was itself spotted by the radars of the convoy's escorts that then went to 'action stations'. The Junkers then flew twice across the stern of the convoy at a range of about eight miles.

Left: Lt Erik Erikson walks across HMS *Biter*'s deck after his successful engagement of the Ju 290. (F. C. Lennox via Mrs M. Sanderson)

Right: Lt Bill Dimes after landing back aboard following the successful intercept. (F. C. Lennox via Mrs M. Sanderson)

Aboard HMS *Biter* the duty pilots of 811 Squadron's Fighter Flight that morning were Lts William Dimes and Erik Erikson, both members of the RNZNVR, who quickly warmed the engines of their Wildcats and prepared for action. Shortly afterwards the order to launch was given and Dimes powered off in Wildcat IV FN252/R closely followed by Erikson at the controls of FN168/Q. Once safely airborne they were given vectors by *Biter*'s air director Lt Francis Pagen towards the intruder that appeared to be setting up for an attack with glider bombs. Shortly after 1100hrs following Pagen's radioed instructions the two fighters closed on the huge Junkers. They were spotted by the German crew who desperately then sought cloud cover, but to no avail. Erikson attacked first through a barrage of defensive cannon fire and before the Junkers reached cloud had succeeded in shooting out one of the starboard engines. At the same time, Lt Dimes was attempting to draw off fire whilst Erikson made his attack. The two fighters then held off and Lt Erikson correctly anticipated where the intruder would come out of the cloud. When it did so he was able to re-engage and '9V+FH' fell into the sea and exploded just beyond the convoy, its demise being cheered by the seamen. This was 811 Squadron Fighter Flight's only successful engagement.

Taken from the deck of HMS *Biter* at 1105hrs the smoke marks the demise of Ltn Elfert's Ju 290 after it had been shot down by Lt Erik Erikson. (F. C. Lennox via Mrs M. Sanderson)

Due to the weather both Erik Erikson and Bill Dimes had difficulty landing back onto *Biter*'s pitching deck but eventually recovered their Wildcats safely aboard. Subsequently, Lt Erikson was awarded the DSC and Dimes and all the fighter direction team were mentioned in despatches.

However, the day was not over for *Biter*'s air direction team of WO (A) Stanley Brown and LA (R) Percy Clipsham led by Lt Pagen. Later on they detected Hptm Bergen's Ju 290 and vectored an escorting Beaufighter from Northern Ireland-based 235 Squadron to intercept '9V+DK' which was also shot down. There were no survivors from either crew from FAGr 5's second fatal encounter of the day.

Wildcat IV FN168/Q that has nosed over on the pitching deck of HMS *Biter* was the aircraft flown by Lt Erikson in his successful engagement. (F. C. Lennox via Mrs M. Sanderson)

# CAPE WICKETKEEPER
# 11 March 1944

The closure of shipping routes from India and Australasia via the Suez Canal and Mediterranean resulted in most sea traffic routing via the Cape of Good Hope. This was recognised by the German naval high command that sent small but significant numbers of U-boats to the South Atlantic and Indian Ocean. The sole RAF Catalina flying boat unit permanently based in South Africa was 262 Squadron which was established with Catalinas at Congella in Durban harbour during early 1943. It later extended its operations to the waters around the Cape of Good Hope establishing an advanced base at Saldanha Bay at Langebaan, 75 miles north of Cape Town. In November, the squadron came under the control of the SAAF Coastal Area Command.

Flt Lt 'Gar' Nash, seated second from left and his crew who made the attack that sank *UIT-22*.
(E. S. S. Nash)

Seen from Fg Off Surridge's aircraft, Flt Lt Nash's crew in Catalina Ib FP174/P makes its attack run on *UIT-22* in the face of heavy fire that can be seen splashing around the aircraft. (A. H. Surridge)

In early March 1944, naval intelligence at Combined HQ in Cape Town indicated that two U-boats were to rendezvous in the waters south of Cape Town so initiating Operation Wicketkeeper to destroy them. In response 262 Squadron moved seven Catalinas down to Langebaan as the submarines' radio transmissions were tracked by Allied radio direction finders (RDF). The operation began on 8 March with Flt Lt A. M. Fletcher's crew in Catalina Ib FP226/J completing an uneventful 15-hour search repeated by two crews the next day.

From 0420hrs on 11 March three 262 Squadron crews captained by Flt Lt Fred Roddick RCAF in FP279/D, Fg Off Oscar Surridge (in FP251/A) and Flt Lt 'Gar' Nash (FP174/P) left Langebaan and headed south. They were on pre-briefed routes to intercept the U-boats that were heading for a rendezvous about 600 miles south of Cape Town. Roddick flew the westerly track, Surridge the easterly with Nash in the centre. It was almost six hours' flying to the patrol area though during the transit the primus cooker in the galley of Nash's aircraft burst into flames burning the face of Sgt Ted Walker. He was treated and placed into the bunk just as the alarm sounded as a 'flash' sighting report had been received from Roddick's aircraft. Flt Lt Nash later recalled: "I remember the Morse signal SSS – SSS on the morning of 11 March, signalling that Flt Lt Roddick in Catalina 'D' was making his attack on a U-boat far south of our Catalina."

At 1048hrs Flt Lt Roddick's crew had spotted the U-boat on the surface 585 miles from Langebaan. The submarine was cruising at ten knots on a westerly course. With Sgt Bill Hill firing the nose guns as they made their run, Roddick attacked in the face of

The *UIT-22* emerges from the spray of the initial attack by Flt Lt Roddick's crew that caused grievous damage. (F. J. Roddick)

heavy fire from the submarine and he dropped five 250lb depth charges that straddled the vessel. The Catalina crew saw the sea erupt around the submarine that immediately took on a list to starboard. Roddick then climbed to 200 feet and positioned for a second run to drop a hung-up depth charge which successfully released and exploded five yards from the bow. Clearly badly damaged, 12 minutes after the initial attack the vessel submerged. The flying boat crew dropped a smoke float to mark the datum but Roddick's Catalina had been severely damaged by the U-boat's 20mm and 37mm cannon fire. The aircraft's port wing and the float mechanism were damaged and the starboard engine was leaking oil. Shortly after 1130hrs Nash's crew arrived at the scene and relieved the damaged aircraft that then departed. Debris and an oil slick on the surface where the U-boat had submerged were evidence of the effectiveness of the attack by Roddick's crew.

Flt Lt Nash later recalled: "To my amazement, the U-boat surfaced in front of my eyes!" He set his crew up to attack the obviously crippled vessel as the third aircraft flown by Flt Lt Surridge's crew had by now also arrived on the scene. Surridge flew a parallel course and covered Nash's aircraft with machine-gun fire as it attacked in the face of heavy fire from the submarine. Gar Nash continued:

"Tommy Tromans in the bow turret opened up with his twin 0.3-inch Vickers machine gun. I could see the conning tower of the U-boat clearly, and dropped all six 250lb depth charges from a height of only 75 feet. It was a perfect straddle. The depth charges exploded beneath the water's surface and the U-boat sank under the waves. It was a formidable adversary."

The attack had shattered the submarine which disappeared in a welter of foam, oil and debris. After a further ten minutes a bubble of thicker, darker oil rose to the surface as *UIT-22* went down taking with it Oltn zur See Karl Wunderlich and his crew. It was the final U-boat sinking in South African waters.

The explosions from the depth charges dropped by Flt Lt Nash's crew fatally envelop the *UIT-22*. (B. Hanson)

Despite the stormy weather, both crews remained in the area in case the submarine should resurface. At 1400hrs Nash's crew set course for Langebaan where they alighted at 1725hrs after 13 hours in the air while Surridge's crew continued the search with a destroyer until 1730hrs. They then also set course for base to celebrate with the other crews along with copious beer and *braaivleis*. In April Flt Lt Roddick received the DFC for his actions.

Fg Off Oscar Surridge, seated second from the left and his crew covered Nash's fatal attack with gunfire and took the remarkable pictures of the action. (A. H. Surridge)

# NUREMBERG NIGHTMARE
# 30 March 1944

In November 1943 Bomber Command began a series of heavy attacks on the German capital that became known as the Battle of Berlin. As well as Berlin, through the winter raids were also mounted against other cities despite at times suffering near crippling losses. On 30 March the city of Nuremberg in Bavaria was the selected target for almost 800 heavy bombers and among the participating units was 51 Squadron at Snaith that flew the Halifax III.

In the absence of the CO at around 1830hrs on 30 March one of 51 Squadron's flight commanders, Sqn Ldr Peter Hill, opened the briefing with the words: "Gentlemen, your target for tonight is Nuremberg." By chance, HQ Bomber Command had selected that night to invite a party of press reporters to Snaith to view the preparations for a raid and they attended the brief with 119 aircrew. The crews voiced concerns about the selected

Sqn Ldr Peter Hill of 51 Squadron briefs his crews at Snaith on the afternoon of 30 March but within a few hours he would be dead as would 34 others in the room and seven others were prisoners. (51 Squadron Records)

Sqn Ldr Paul Jousse the squadron's senior navigator helps Fg Off Harry Bowling prepare for his first operation. It was also his last as he was killed near Neustadt with most of Flt Sgt Brougham's crew. (51 Squadron Records)

route while an additional worry was that 51 Squadron was in the last wave to bomb – often the most vulnerable.

At exactly 2200hrs, Flt Sgt Ted Wilkins, an Australian, eased Halifax III LV522/MH-Z off Snaith's runway on the crew's sixth operation, followed two minutes later by W/O Hayes at the controls of LW522/MH-J. Fifteen more Halifaxes followed them with Sqn Ldr Hill, who was flying with a scratch crew, being the sixth off. Last to depart was Flt Sgt Sarjantson's crew though en route two aircraft were forced to abort with technical problems. The remainder headed into Germany with the bomber stream but by ill fortune the Germans were marshalling their night fighters at two radio beacons near Aachen and Frankfurt that were immediately adjacent to the selected route. Natural factors also conspired as the winds were markedly different from those forecast while the anticipated cloud cover never materialised. The clear, cold skies also caused many bombers to stream condensation trails – a deadly marker for the waiting night fighters. Soon there was a steady stream of blazing wreckage along the route.

The first 51 Squadron aircraft to fall was that of Flt Sgt Wilkins shot down by a night fighter near Wetzlar; there were no survivors. They were soon followed by LW544 flown by Flt Sgt Geoff Brougham's crew that comprised five Australians and two Englishmen. Shortly before 0100hrs when at 19,000 feet they were attacked by a night fighter, possibly the Messerschmitt Bf 110G of Oblt Martin Becker of 6./NJG 3. Badly hit, the Halifax began spinning on fire and only Sgt Williams the bomb aimer and Flt Sgt Gowland the flight engineer baled out. Becker may also have shot down Sgt Binder's crew who came down near Rossbach, again without survivors. Soon afterwards a little further to the east Flt Sgt Malcolm Stembridge's crew became 51 Squadron's fourth loss. He was one of two of the crew who died when the Halifax crashed near Fladungen, possibly the victim of Ltn Hans Raum of 9./NGJ 3.

The bomber stream pressed on and turned south toward the target, though the effects of the unknown 'jet stream' meant many were well off course. Perversely, as they approached Nuremberg the longed-for cloud cover appeared and obscured the

Halifax III LV777/MH-F lands at Snaith after its pre-op air test but was shot down by flak near Stuttgart with the loss of Sqn Ldr Hill's crew later that night. (51 Squadron Records)

At Snaith anxious eyes are cast to the skies awaiting the return of some of 51's overdue aircraft. The station commander, Gp Capt Fresson is on the balcony. (51 Squadron Records)

target. At 0115hrs on the 31st Sgt Duckworth's bomb aimer, Flt Sgt Muir released their load over the target just as they were attacked by a Ju 88 which the gunners drove off. Flt Sgt Sarjantson's crew also bombed at the same time and both crews gratefully headed for home. Over the next ten minutes the Halifaxes skippered by Flt Lt Pawell and Flt Sgts Davies, Pettifer, Hall and Norton all unleashed their loads from 19,000ft seeing an intense glow of fires through the clouds. Plt Off Mike O'Loughlin's crew also bombed and set course for home having noted a considerable amount of fighter activity. Sadly, the main attack on Nuremberg itself was a failure as the city was unexpectedly covered by thick cloud and creep back to the attack thus developed and many bombs fell into open country to the north.

By then 11 51 Squadron Halifaxes were heading home on the planned route avoiding known defences. However, some aircraft that were uncertain of their position overflew the heavily defended area of Stuttgart. Among them was Halifax III LV777/MH-F flown by Sqn Ldr Peter Hill which was shot down by flak at Bietigheim, just north of the city and there were no survivors.

For the surviving ten crews the flight back was uneventful and shortly after 0500hrs Sgt Duckworth brought LW364/MH-B down onto Snaith's runway, the first to return. Fifteen minutes later Flt Lt Pawell's crew arrived followed at 0615hrs by Mike O'Loughlin's Halifax. Six others had landed elsewhere but LW579 flown Plt Off J. Brooks crashed near Stokenchurch in Buckinghamshire and there were no survivors.

In total 95 bombers were missing and ten more crashed in England on return. In Bomber Command's worst night 51 Squadron lost six of the 17 Halifaxes despatched, a staggering 35 per cent that was proportionately the greatest of the night. Of the 119 aircrew at the briefing 35 were dead and seven others were POWs.

The nightmare at Nuremberg was the nadir of 51 Squadron's war.

At debriefing in the early hours of 31 March the strain is evident on the faces of Plt Off Mike O'Loughlin's crew that was one of only three to return to Snaith. (51 Squadron Records)

# A UNIQUE DOUBLE
# 8 June 1944

The huge armada of shipping off the French coast during the D-Day landings was highly vulnerable to attack from the sea and responsibility for the safety of the landing forces fell in large part to RAF Coastal Command whose aircraft flew day and night 'Cork' patrols. When the landings were confirmed, the German naval HQ ordered all available submarines from their French bases to join those already at sea to attack the invasion fleet. Thus 42 U-boats in all were attempting to reach the English Channel.

Two of the submarines were Oblt Detlef von Lehsten's *U-373* and *U-441* under KptLt Klaus Hartmann that at about 0200hrs on 8 June were both on the surface, a few miles apart, some 50 miles west of the French coast. In the area on patrol at 500ft was Liberator GR V BZ792/2-G of 224 Squadron captained by a Canadian, Flt Lt Kenneth O. 'Kayo' Moore which had taken off from St Eval, Cornwall shortly after 2200hrs on 7 June. With

After landing Moore's crew were met by a photographer to record those that had flown this unique sortie. Rear from left to right: W/O Jock MacDowall, Flt Sgt I. C. Webb, Fg Off J. M. Ketcheson, W/O Ernie Davison, Sgt John Hamer and W/O D. H. Greise. Front from left to right: Plt Off Al Gibb, W/O Mike Werbinski, Fg Off 'Kayo' Moore and W/O Peter Foster. (RAF St Eval Records via R. C. B. Ashworth)

During their successful sortie the Moore crew flew in a Liberator GR V armed with a dozen depth charges and a homing torpedo. (RAF St Eval Records via R. C. B. Ashworth)

him were co-pilot Fg Off J. M. Ketcheson, navigators Plt Off Al Gibb and W/O Johnston 'Jock' MacDowall, flight engineer Sgt John Hamer and wireless operator/air gunners W/Os Ernie Davison, Peter Foster, Mike Werbinski, D. H. Greise and Flt Sgt I. C. Webb. They also carried their mascot, 'Dinty', a stuffed panda. The Liberator was armed with a dozen 250lb Torpex depth charges and a single 600lb acoustic torpedo. It was one of six sorties flown by 224 Squadron that night.

At 0210hrs W/O Foster gained a radar contact and Moore positioned the Liberator up the moon path. At a range of three miles in near perfect visibility they spotted a fully surfaced U-boat, probably *U-441*. Moore's report described the subsequent events:

"It was a perfect silhouette, as if it were painted on white paper, and I could make out the conning tower perfectly. As we approached at 40ft height we could see the U-boat's crew had been taken by surprise. About eight German sailors on deck, apparently in utter confusion, were running like hell to man their guns. The U-boat commander, however, made no attempt to crash dive, and those manning the guns waited for us to close the range. Al Gibb, our front gunner, opened fire when we were within 1,000 yards and scored repeated hits on the conning tower and deck. Simultaneously the Germans opened fire on us. I took evasive action while Gibb continued to blaze away, and then tracked over the conning tower. The flak had been

Fg Off Moore and his navigator W/O MacDowall in front of their Liberator GR V at St Eval after their epic sortie. (K. O. Moore via D. O'Malley)

silenced during the last yards, and we released our depth charges in a perfect straddle. I saw one of the crew in the 'bandstand' double up and fall overboard into the water. The U-boat seemed to jump into the air and explode, splitting wide open. I made a steep turn. On the water we could see wreckage and large patches of oil. As we stooged around for another five minutes we saw black objects in the water, probably bodies."

The crew were understandably thrilled, but with weapons still in the bomb bay they remained on task though their excitement was not over. At 2040hrs there was further action as Moore's report continued:

"Almost immediately W/O MacDowall, the navigator, who at the time was adjusting the bomb sight, shouted a warning that he could see another U-boat ahead, travelling fairly slowly. It was a small U-boat and remained fully surfaced, making no attempt to avoid a fight. As we closed to attack Al Gibb opened up from the front turret and we met heavy flak, which came up in the shape of a coloured fan. Going straight through all this we roared over the conning tower and dropped the remaining DCs, getting a perfect straddle according to my rear gunner. After this run the U-boat was still on the surface but listing heavily to starboard. As we circled I saw the bow of the U-boat rise 25 feet out of the water at a 75-degree angle, then slide back into the sea. We made a third circuit over the spot where the U-boat had vanished. Three dinghies were in the water with three or four sailors in each, then we resumed our patrol."

They had attacked *U-373* and among the 47 survivors was its captain though after the earlier attack *U-441* had gone down with all hands. In the space of less than 30 minutes Moore and his crew had scored a unique achievement by sinking more than one U-boat in a single sortie. This feat was quickly recognised when 'Kayo' Moore received an immediate DSO, while his navigator, W/O Johnston MacDowall and wireless operator W/O Peter Foster received DFCs and the flight engineer, Sgt John Hamer, was decorated with the DFM.

The signal congratulating Fg Off Moore on the immediate award of the DSO. (K. O. Moore via D. O'Malley)

# SUPPORTING THE SCOUTS
# 27 June 1944

At the start of WW2 the nascent Indian Air Force began expanding to assume greater responsibility for the defence of India from the RAF. One of the newly formed units was 3 Squadron that was formed in October 1941 for army co-operation and aerial policing duties on the fractious North-West Frontier Province (NWFP) of India. Despite the threat of the Japanese on the eastern borders of India, it was Air HQ policy to maintain two IAF squadrons on the NWFP to which 3 Squadron rotated regularly on 'watch and ward' operations. In September 1943 when under Sqn Ldr Prithipal Singh re-equipment with 16 Hurricane IIcs began and in November the squadron moved first to Phaphamau then Ranchi for gunnery training before returning to Kohat on the frontier in February.

In mid-April 1944, 3 Squadron moved a detachment south-west to Miranshah in the mountains of the North-West Frontier Province close to the border with Afghanistan, relieving 1 Squadron from watch and ward duties. Within days of arriving action against the warring Pathan tribes resumed when on 13 April 3 Squadron flew 32 bombing sorties against prescribed targets during which 64 250lb bombs were dropped. However, near Dosali Fort on the 14th when returning from

the sixth raid of the day, Fg Off Pratap Lal Singh in Hurricane LA128 and Fg Off d'Eca in LD371 collided and crashed. Lal was killed but d'Eca baled out and was rescued by the Tochi Scouts they had been supporting.

During the intense period of action in late June Sqn Ldr Prithipal Singh (right) personally led half the sorties. (Air Mshl Vikram Singh)

Flt Lt Dalap Singh Majithia was the A Flight commander who led the first attack on 27 June and was active through the period. (Air Mshl Vikram Singh)

June became the squadron's busiest month on the NWFP flying tactical recces, direct support including supply dropping and some artillery spotting. However, during the last four days of the month there was an intensive period of bombing around Marghai when rebel guns opened fire on the fort at Ghariom manned by the Tochi Scouts, killing one of the Scouts. Early on 26 June Flt Lt Dalap Singh Majithia the A Flight commander flew Maj Venning of the Scouts in the Harvard in an attempt to locate the guns. That evening he and Fg Off Archie David in Hurricanes flew two sorties to again look for the guns and drop warning leaflets to the tribesmen.

At 0650hrs the following morning Flt Lt Majithia led four Hurricanes on a prescription bombing attack against Marghai. As they landed at 0725hrs Sqn Ldr Prithipal Singh took off in Hurricane IIc LA109 leading Fg Off Dilip Kumar Bose in KZ371/R in a repeat attack with 500lb bombs on the target. However, Fg Off Bose suffered a bomb hang-up that he finally managed to jettison

During the intensive period of bombing at Marghai in support of the Tochi Scouts on 27 June 1944, Hurricane IIC KZ371/R was flown three times by Fg Off Dilip Kumar Bose. On the first occasion he suffered a bomb hang-up. (Air Mshl Vikram Singh)

over Miranshah range. The CO photographed Bose's aircraft before the pair landed at 0815hrs. There were six waves of bombing sorties through the day despite the poor visibility with Fg Off Bose flying KZ371 again in the third wave that was led by the CO when the four Hurricanes reported several direct hits. Dilip Bose flew KZ371 as No. 3 when the CO again led the day's penultimate wave when six direct hits were made; this was the aircraft's last sortie until the 30th. These attacks were all made in the face of intense small-arms fire which damaged Hurricane LD112 flown by Fg Off Om Prakash Mehra in the starboard wing, though he landed it safely.

There was then a pause of several hours but in late afternoon two single sorties flown by Fg Off Randhir Singh and Fg Off B. A. Hall were scrambled on a call from the Tochi Scouts and the former strafed a gun position in a cave outside which a number of tribesmen had been seen; several casualties were claimed. Finally, at 1930hrs two four-aircraft sections led by the CO and Flt Lt Majithia attacked the cave gun position and bombs were dropped from 1,500ft after dive attacks.

The bombing continued the next day and later in the day several spotting sorties were made to support the artillery while Flt Lt Majithia and Fg Off Bose flew recces in the Harvard to assess the damage from the bombing. After a recce in support of the advancing column of the Razmak Brigade on 29 June four more bombing sorties were made against the nominated target. Five more attacks, four of them led by the CO, were made on the 30th that brought 3 Squadron's most intense period of operations to date to an end. Sqn Ldr Singh had personally led half the missions during this intense period of activity.

The trouble subsided thereafter and the frontier returned to a restless calm.

The 3 Squadron Harvard IIB was occasionally used for reconnaissance over the NWFP, often carrying an army officer. (Air Mshl Vikram Singh)

# A BRIDGE TOO FAR
# 17 September 1944

By mid-August 1944 the Allied armies finally shattered the German 7th Army and broke out from Normandy. Over the next three weeks they advanced at breakneck speed and by early September paused in Belgium on the Dutch border. After several aborted operations Operation Market Garden was proposed that would deliver the First Allied Airborne Army to capture key bridges across the major waterways in the Netherlands. Coincident with this would be a ground advance across the bridges and so turning the defences of the Siegfried Line. The British 1st Airborne Division was to capture the bridge across the Lower Rhine at Arnhem that was the most distant objective, 60 miles behind enemy lines. The division would be delivered onto drop zones (DZs) at Wolfheze, north-west of Arnhem. The huge force would require three lifts by RAF and USAAF transports and gliders flying in daylight, albeit under heavy escort. One of the RAF transport units was 620 Squadron at Fairford, Gloucestershire under Wg Cdr Donald Lee flying Stirling IVs equipped for paradrop and glider towing.

Paratroopers from the pathfinders of the 21st Independent Parachute Company prepare to board Stirlings of 620 Squadron at Fairford on the morning of 17 September. (R. S. G. Mackay)

Just before midday on 17 September a 620 Squadron Stirling IV lifts off from Fairford towing its Horsa glider en route to Arnhem. (N. R. Chaffey)

For the first lift 620 Squadron had to allocate six aircraft, with a similar number from 190 Squadron, to drop the pathfinders of the 21st Independent Parachute Company under Maj 'Boy' Wilson, who were to mark the landing zones half an hour in advance of the main lift. Sqn Ldr Richard Bunker began 620's part in the operation when at 1010hrs he lifted Stirling IV LJ930 off carrying the pathfinders followed by those flown by Flt Lt Jack, Fg Off Kay, Flt Lt Hannah, Fg Off Bunce and Plt Off McKenzie.

Thirty-five minutes later the squadron's remaining 19 Stirlings began taking off at one-minute intervals each hauling a heavily laden Airspeed Horsa glider off Fairford's runway. W/O Miller in LJ980, W/O Keogh in LJ918 and Fg Off Marshall flying LK116 were the first off. The squadron then began forming up and heading east at 2,500 feet. However, the tow ropes of the gliders pulled by Fg Off Gawith flying Stirling IV LJ873/QS-H and Plt Off Kidgall (LJ875) broke when still over England and the tugs returned to Fairford, landing at 1120hrs and 1140hrs. The remainder of 620 Squadron's combinations continued towards the coastal rendezvous at Aldeburgh on the Suffolk coast where other formations from Keevil and Harwell joined to form a 'train' of over 120 Stirling/Horsa combinations.

The aerial armada continued almost without incident other than several tows casting off and over the Dutch coast at West Schouwen they met with the fighter escort for the run in to the DZs. As the main force ran north towards Arnhem, at 1240hrs the first of the 89 pathfinders jumped from 620 Squadron's six Stirlings; the remainder jumped from 190 Squadron. The drop was a complete success and

Ground crew prepare Stirling IV LJ566/QS-E for Flt Lt Gordon Thring's crew to depart for Arnhem on the first lift. (N. R. Chaffey)

was achieved without loss and these men then marked the DZs on the heathland at Wolfheze for the incoming waves of Dakotas, Stirlings and gliders.

The remaining 17 of 620's aircraft then ran in with the first wave as planned, towing Horsas loaded with men, Jeeps, trailers, motorcycles and anti-tank guns of the 1st

Led by Wg Cdr Lee the CO in LJ847/QS-X, Stirlings of 620 Squadron return from Arnhem on the first day. The nearest aircraft is LJ566/QS-E flown by Flt Lt Gordon Thring. (Fordyce Collection)

Airlanding Brigade. The tow on the glider behind one of the squadron's Stirlings was hit by some of the very little ground fire encountered over the continent and the glider parted. However, the remaining 16 ran in towards Arnhem with little enemy reaction. To the surprise and relief of the squadron's crews who were more generally used to night operations, there was little enemy fire, much of which had been neutralised by the 2nd TAF fighters. Such opposition as was encountered was promptly dealt with by the plethora of escorts. Approaching Wolfheze at about 1310hrs the crews released their Horsas which then flew down onto LZ 'S', whilst now disencumbered the Stirlings broke away and climbed out and headed home in boxes of four. Wg Cdr Lee in LJ847/QS-X led one section that comprised QS-R, QS-Q and LJ566/QS-E (flown by Flt Lt Gordon Thring).

At 1440hrs Sqn Ldr Bunker was the first of the pathfinder group to return to Fairford, soon followed by the first of the 620 Squadron main force of glider tugs. From the squadron's perspective the lift had been a complete success. One of the aircraft had carried a group of war correspondents, who gave glowing though not entirely accurate accounts of their experiences.

At Fairford and elsewhere the aircraft were prepared for the next lift with 300 more gliders made ready. Although the airborne assault had achieved surprise, the ground advance was soon behind schedule and the first bridge at Grave was not secured until 19 September. By then there was heavy fighting around the bridges at Nijmegen and at Arnhem around which, unknown to the Allies, two SS Panzer Divisions had been refitting. Ominously, at Arnhem the 1st Airborne Division was already out of contact. With surprise now lost, over succeeding days the transports suffered crippling losses trying to resupply the beleaguered paras with 620 Squadron losing five crews, including that of the CO, though he survived.

# THUMBS UP!
# 6 January 1945

At the beginning of 1945 the Canadian-manned 420 Squadron was based at Tholthorpe in the Vale of York, 13 miles north-west of the city and was commanded by Wg Cdr William Gerald Phelan. The squadron was equipped with the Halifax III as part of 6 Group, Bomber Command conducting the night-bombing offensive against Germany. The skipper of one of the

**Left:** Fg Off William Anderson, the 22-year-old pilot of Halifax III NA179/PT-B. (Anderson Family)

**Below:** Fg Off William Anderson receives a 'thumbs up' from Rev Sqn Ldr E. S. Light as he taxies Halifax III NA179/PT-B of 420 Squadron for an attack on Hanau on 6 January 1945. (DND/RCAF)

squadron crews was 22-year-old Fg Off William Anderson from Toronto who before volunteering for the Royal Canadian Air Force had worked at the Ogilvie flour mills. He enlisted in September 1942 and trained at several flying schools, graduating as a pilot on 28 January 1944 before sailing for England. There he was posted to Bomber Command, completing further training at Operational Training and Heavy Conversion Units forming his crew who in late 1944 joined 420 Squadron. The crew was allocated Halifax III NA179/PT-B.

On 6 January 1945, an official Canadian photographer visited Tholthorpe and on the airfield the station padre, the Rev Sqn Ldr E. S. Light, posed for a famous photograph giving a traditional 'thumbs up' signal as William Anderson taxied past at the controls of NA179 before departing for a raid on Hanau, a few miles east of Frankfurt. They were part of a raid of almost 500 heavy bombers drawn from 1, 4, 6 and 8 Groups and was aimed at the important railway junctions and rail sidings in the town, around 40 per cent of which was destroyed. Despite the still formidable night defences only four Halifaxes and two Lancasters were lost, none of which were from 420 Squadron. By the time the photograph was taken the crew had already flown several operations over Germany, including attacks on Cologne and Ludwigshafen.

On 28 January Wg Cdr F. S. McCarthy took over command of 420 Squadron that on 14 February allocated nine of its Halifaxes towards the 6 Group contribution of 66 Halifaxes and 52 Lancasters to the force of over 700 aircraft of Bomber Command in an attack on the town of Chemnitz in Lower Saxony. At Tholthorpe 420 Squadron's ground crews filled the nine aircraft with the maximum fuel load to take them deep into eastern Germany and loaded each with a dozen 500lb MC bombs. The weather

was forecast to be cloudy and at the briefing the bombing height was specified at 19,000 to 19,500ft at 2100hrs. Having been briefed William Anderson and his crew of Sgt Harry Evans who was RAF, and fellow Canadians Fg Offs John Sinden, Lloyd Jones and Stanley

Wg Cdr Bill Phelan (right) was the CO of 420 Squadron when Anderson's crew arrived and two weeks before their loss, he was replaced by Wg Cdr F. S. McCarthy (left). (DND/RCAF)

The seven men of Fg Off William Anderson's crew, six of whom died on 14 February 1945. (Anderson Family)

Hay, Plt Off Earl Sills and Flt Sgt W. H. Giles jumped aboard the transport that took them out to dispersal where they clambered aboard NA179. They started up and followed the other Halifaxes to the runway and having been given a green light from the runway caravan controller with Evans following him through on the throttles, Anderson put on maximum power on the four Hercules engines and the heavily laden aircraft left Tholthorpe's runway at 1701hrs. It was their ninth operation.

The nine heavily laden Halifaxes climbed slowly to altitude and set their course out over the North Sea for eastern Germany. However, having settled into the cruise, around about an hour and a half later the starboard outer engine of NA179 caught fire. Harry Evans the flight engineer activated the fire extinguisher and William Anderson shut the engine down and feathered the propeller. The crew then sent a radio message to Tholthorpe informing them of the problem and that they were returning to base. Having returned safely to Yorkshire shortly after 2000hrs NA179 joined Tholthorpe's landing circuit and Anderson descended it to 600ft before turning onto final approach. What happened next is unclear but eyewitnesses saw the aircraft enter a spin then fall out of control and crash a mile south-west of the airfield near the village of Alne close to the York-to-Darlington railway line. When rescuers reached the aircraft, they found Flt Sgt Giles the 19-year-old mid-upper gunner had somehow survived, but that Fg Off Anderson and the rest of his crew had been killed.

The only Englishman on board, Sgt Evans, was buried by his family at Whiston near Liverpool whilst the five Canadians were laid to rest in Harrogate Cemetery. They were among 336 men lost by 420 Squadron, mute reminders that not all of Bomber Command's casualties were victims of the Luftwaffe.

# NO ESCAPE
# 22 May 1945

In late 1943 203 Squadron, a long-serving Middle East-based unit had moved to India and re-equipped with Wellingtons for patrol duties over the Bay of Bengal. In October 1944 it had moved to Madura where the following month it began conversion to the Liberator GR VI and became operational before the end of the year. In February 1945 the squadron moved to Kankesanturai, Ceylon, resuming operations in the anti-shipping role the following month. Commanded by Wg Cdr Cedric Masterman the squadron flew its first sortie in this new role that was mounted over huge distances on 20 March resulting in a coaster being sunk.

Sqn Ldr Percy Waddy (seated centre) and his crew in front of Liberator KH289/B 'Peggy II' in which they made their effective attack on 22 May 1945. (S. A. Wheeler)

As Percy Waddy's Liberator closes in, this photograph shows the Japanese coaster being hit by fire from the nose turret moments before the bombs were released. (S. A. Wheeler)

A few days later there came a 'flap' following reports that a Japanese Myōkō-class heavy cruiser had been seen heading for the Nicobar Islands but despite extensive searches nothing was seen. However there then came reports of numerous small cargo ships, code named 'Sugar Dogs', conducting resupply around the islands and an attack was planned. On the 22nd Sqn Ldr Percy Waddy, the Canadian flight commander, and his crew in Liberator GR VI KH289/B named 'Peggy II' lifted off from Kankesanturai at 0713hrs. They were followed by three more crews skippered by Flt Lt Aldcroft flying KH955, Flt Lt Fletcher in KG849 and KH307 flown by Fg Off Law to conduct a parallel track anti-shipping sweep east of Great Nicobar.

Three of the aircraft were carrying 250lb bombs with 11-second delay fuses whilst the fourth (KG849), by way of experiment, carried depth charges. Arriving in the area at shortly before 1400hrs the Liberators flew at just 50ft. Fletcher's crew sighted two coasters of approximately 120 and 90ft in length on course 310 degrees. He attacked the smaller of these with the depth charges and obtained a straddle from 50ft. The attack was most effective as the ship appeared to be blown out of the water and disintegrated under the force of the explosion, sinking almost immediately leaving much debris in the water in position 0640 9400E. However, return fire had hit the aircraft wounding the navigator, Fg Off Partridge.

Flt Lt Aldcroft set up for an attack on the larger vessel only to suffer the frustration of having his bombs hang up due to an electrical problem. In the third aircraft Fg Off Law then attacked but the bombs were released prematurely. By which time Percy Waddy had swung Peggy II in to attack with Sgt Sawyer the nose gunner smothering the vessel in .50in machine-gun fire as they ran in. Waddy accurately dropped eight bombs scoring direct hits and almost immediately the ship burst into flames following an explosion amidships. Waddy then circled the aircraft for the crew

The wreckage of the Japanese-manned coaster sunk by Sqn Ldr Waddy's crew off the coast of Siam a month later on, on 23 June. (S. A. Wheeler)

to take photographs, whilst the ship burnt fiercely emitting clouds of black smoke. Photographs showed the cargo as including oil drums. After the ship had sunk, some survivors were seen in the water, but no rafts nor ships boats were seen.

Flying as a wireless operator/mechanic (WOM) in the crew was Flt Sgt Stan Wheeler who recalled the attack:

"We in Percy Waddy's crew had our success on 22 May 1945. Four aircraft were on the anti-shipping sweep and when we arrived the convoy was under attack. We saw Law's aircraft do his run but his bombs dropped early, not just short. We dived in and dropped ours and our camera showed our bombs actually going in."

For the unfortunate Japanese crew there had been no escape, neither was there a month later when the same crew destroyed another 'Sugar Dog' off Paknam, Siam on 23 June.

Liberator GR VI KG911/D in dispersal at Kankesanturai in which Percy Waddy's crew made a further sinking on 23 June. (S. A. Wheeler)

# FIRST SEAFIRE OVER JAPAN
# 17 July 1945

As the British Pacific Fleet (BPF) prepared at its base in Australia for operations off Japan, it was joined by the new armoured carrier HMS *Implacable* whose fighter complement included the Supermarine Seafires of 801 and 880 Squadrons. The latter was commanded by Lt Cdr Mike Crosley with Lt Norman Goodfellow as senior pilot. As it had not participated in the Okinawa operations, as a final work-up for the ship, in mid-June *Implacable*'s Air Group raided the bypassed Japanese base at Truk in the Caroline Islands. The ship then sailed from the BPF's forward base at Manus to join *Formidable*, *Victorious* and *Indefatigable* before sailing for Japanese waters.

There had been much concern that the Seafire's short range might limit its use to defensive combat air patrols (CAP) over the Fleet rather than offensive work. However, at Manus a consignment of P-40 Kittyhawk drop tanks was identified and 'acquired' in an arrangement with the Americans involving a quantity of gin. Carried beneath the fuselage, the drop tanks increased the range of the Seafire considerably

The first pilot to fly a Seafire over Japan was 880 Squadron's senior pilot, Lt Norman Goodfellow. (Author's Collection)

as the CO of 880 Squadron Lt Cdr Crosley wrote: "The end result was a great boost in the Seafire's operational endurance to three and a half hours. Suddenly, it was capable of engaging in Ramrod offensive air superiority missions."

Aircraft from the US Navy Task Force 38 began operations over the Japanese Home Islands on 14 July and were then joined by the BPF (TF 37) though the first act was to fly formations of Seafires and Fireflies over the US Fleet to familiarise them with the new aircraft. With their better climb performance, initially the Seafires were to be used for defensive CAP against the anticipated Japanese kamikaze attacks, though it was anticipated they would also be used to escort Avenger bombers

The CO photographed the first Seafire to fly over Japan on 17 July, though the strike was cancelled due to heavy fog. (R. M. Crosley)

and in making ground attacks. At 0530hrs on 17 July HMS *Implacable* began operations when it launched a dozen 880 Squadron Seafires in three sections led by Sub-Lt Pye, Lt Simpson and Sub-Lt Dancaster for CAP over the Fleet. The ship then launched Seafires of 801 Squadron with Fireflies on Ramrod operations over Japan. However, the mission was recalled due to fog over the coast.

Thus, later in the morning 12 Seafires of 880 Squadron in three sections led by Lt Cdr Crosley, Lt Goodfellow and Lt Yate launched off *Implacable* on a Ramrod. The target was shipping in the harbour at Chōshi, about 60 miles east of Tokyo. Thus, the first Seafires to cross the coast and fly over Japan were from 880 Squadron and the distinction of being the first pilot was Lt Norman Goodfellow who was flying Seafire L III N149. The event was captured for posterity by the CO whose aircraft had been modified and was equipped with an oblique camera. The coastal fog persisted, however, and only the Fireflies were able to locate their targets in the bad weather that covered the target area.

Frustrated, Lt Cdr Crosley who was in NN621/N 115 led the formation back to the ship where on landing-on Sub-Lt 'Legs' Letham put Seafire L III PR126 into *Implacable*'s barrier. In addition to the Ramrod, 880 Squadron mounted three CAPs during the day. Afterwards, the CO voiced the trepidation of all his pilots: "The general sensation of being over Japan was one of foreboding, deep fear. We had heard tales of what the locals did to airmen who got hacked down. We got in and out as quickly as we could."

## PART 3

# POST-WORLD WAR

# KASHMIR ROCKETEERS
# 4 November 1947

At midnight on 14/15 August 1947 India gained independence from Britain with the majority Muslim states joining the newly partitioned state of Pakistan. However, the ruler of the mainly Muslim state of Jammu and Kashmir was undecided to which country to accede. Pre-empting his decision irregular Pathan tribesmen led by regular Pakistan army officers invaded Jammu and Kashmir on 22 October and the local state forces were quickly overwhelmed. Within days the insurgents were just 30 miles from the state capital of Srinagar. On 24 October the Maharaja requested Indian support and signed the Instrument of Accession.

Left: Sqn Ldr Basil Noronha led 7 Squadron during the critical early months of the war and baled out after being hit on 10 December. (via P. V. S. Jagan Mohan)

Right: Flt Lt Randhir Singh who flew the first 7 Squadron sortie over Kashmir. (via P. V. S. Jagan Mohan)

Ground crew load 60lb R/P onto Tempest II PR752 in which Flt Lt Randhir Singh flew strikes around Baramulla on 4 and 6 November. (Air Mshl Vikram Singh)

The Royal Indian Air Force was ill prepared for a war, but 7 Squadron commanded by Sqn Ldr Basil Noronha at Agra with five Tempest IIs and a Harvard was alerted to support 1st Battalion the Sikh Regiment that had been flown into Srinagar and which then established blocking positions. To establish the extent of the insurgents' advance on 27 October two Spitfires flew a reconnaissance over the Baramulla-Srinagar area. They were joined by a Tempest of 7 Squadron flown by Flt Lt Randhir Singh, who was part of a detachment that had moved to Jammu. He was also to assess the air support required to assist the increasingly beleaguered Sikhs.

The following day Randhir Singh and his No. 2 flew a long sortie from Jammu along the Kohala road to the west of Srinagar engaging the tribal insurgent positions at Pattan, 15 miles north-west of the capital with their full loads of 60lb rockets (R/P) and 20mm cannon. This allowed 1st Sikhs to concentrate and establish firmer defensive

On 4 December 1947 Flt Lt Randhir Singh flew Tempest II PR863 on a strike on the Domel tunnel. (Air Mshl Vikram Singh)

Flt Lt Randhir Singh of 7 Squadron flew Tempest HW419 for an air strike at Poonch on 11 December 1947. (D. G. Michael)

positions despite heavy losses. Two days later on 30 October Sqn Ldr Noronha led the rest of his squadron to Ambala and during the day the two aircraft already in place rocketed and strafed insurgents concentrated around Pattan destroying much of their transport. On 3 November the Pathans mounted a surprise attack at Bagdam, just few miles south of Srinagar airfield, though the onslaught was held with the effective air support. On several occasions the Tempests attacked enemy troops just yards from Indian positions and prevented them from being overrun. The main enemy position was identified at Shelatang on the Baramulla Road west of Srinagar on which Flt Lt Randhir Singh in PR752 flew effective rocket attacks on 4 and 6 November. By the 10th the immediate threat to Srinagar had passed then over the next few weeks the squadron flew intensively to halt the insurgents.

The raiders then shifted their focus south-west, to the hill town of Poonch that came under siege. Heavy fighting continued around Uri near where on 1 December the 7 Squadron Harvard flown on a recce by Fg Off Anthony d'Cruz was shot down by ground fire and he and his passenger were captured. Three days later in Tempest II PR863 Flt Lt Randhir Singh participated in a successful attack on the Kohala-to-Domel road tunnel. On the 11th in HW419 he flew a successful R/P attack on insurgents around Poonch.

Ten days later over Jammu Sqn Ldr Noronha's Tempest was hit by insurgent ground fire and he baled out, though was picked up unhurt. The squadron continued to support the army around Uri where among the casualties was Jemadar Nand Singh VC. A few days later Indian troops captured Jangar but the harsh winter weather then forced a halt in major operations that lasted almost three months and brought to an end the first phase of the war.

# THE ACE THAT NEVER WAS
# 13 March 1953

It is generally accepted that a total of five air combat victories gives the successful pilot the accolade of 'ace'. Whilst the claims of most pilots were undoubtedly made in good faith, it is an undoubted fact that claims from all sides were generally inflated, usually by over optimism. Conversely, claims for probables or damaged sometimes actually resulted in the destruction of an aircraft as post-war access to enemy records occasionally reveals. Such was the case of Sqn Ldr Graham Hulse.

When flying Spitfires with 81 Squadron his combat over Sicily with Macchi 202s (in fact Bf 109Gs of II./JG 53) took place on the evening of 14 June 1943, one of which he claimed damaged though three were shot down or crash-landed. Similarly, when flying a 213 Squadron Mustang over Yugoslavia on 23 April 1945 he claimed a Croatian Bf 109G damaged though the aircraft, 'Black 27' flown by Ltn Mihajlo Jelak of 2 Lovacko Jato, was in fact badly hit and crash-landed. More mysteriously, shortly before this on 31 March Hulse was part of a formation of four Spitfires of 94 Squadron led by Sqn Ldr Jack Slade that intercepted a Bf 109 near Salonika and shot it down. At debriefing the markings identified it as Bulgarian and as that nation had just come over to the Allies the action was never formally recorded and only came to light during an interview with one of the surviving Spitfire pilots 50 years later. Thus, officially at the end of WW2 Flt Lt Hulse's score was for two probables and four damaged, though in fact it stood at two and one shared destroyed, one probable and four damaged, an additional damaged claim being uncovered for a combat near Pristina on 12 November 1944 with a Bulgarian Bf 109G flown by Capt Krsto Atanasov.

After the war, Graham Hulse remained in the RAF serving on aerial policing duties in Palestine before training as a flying instructor. However, following the outbreak of the Korean War he volunteered for service there on attachment to the US Air Force.

## MiG ALLEY

In mid-1952 Flt Lt Graham Hulse was seconded to the USAF in Korea and after a two-month conversion to the Canadair-built F-86E Sabre, in September was posted

Sqn Ldr Graham Hulse outside the operations room of the 336th FIS at Kimpo shortly before his loss. (R. Windoffer via W. Thompson)

to the 4th Fighter Interceptor Wing (FIW) at Kimpo, west of the capital Seoul. With his considerable combat experience, he was appointed as C Flight commander. During a sweep over the Yalu River mid-morning on 25 October when flying as No. 4, his element leader, 1/Lt Joseph Fields Jr attacked a MiG-15 that intercepted them. His fire hit the jet in the tail and fuselage before he pulled away. Flt Lt Hulse then closed obtaining further hits resulting in the MiG crashing and exploding near Sinuiju. He was credited with a half share in the victory.

Patrols over the Yalu River, known as 'MiG Alley' continued but his next engagement was not until shortly after midday on 9 December when he was element lead escorting a reconnaissance RF-80A. He spotted two MiG-15s just south of the Yalu and initiated a diving attack onto the camouflaged jets as they climbed through 5,000ft. He quickly overtook the enemy aircraft which pulled into a hard left turn. Hulse closed on one at 8,000ft gaining strikes all over before the pilot was seen to eject and the aircraft crash onto a sandbank near Wonsong-dong.

Sqn Ldr Hulse taxiing for a mission from Kimpo in a 336 FIS F-86E Sabre in early 1953. (W. Thompson)

On 1 January 1953 Graham Hulse was promoted to squadron leader and quickly continued his run of success against Communist jets. On 27 January he was leading a patrol over MiG Alley that was engaged by some MiG-15s at 40,000ft. In a brief engagement he was able to claim one damaged, telling a reporter: "I nipped in behind him at .96 and hit him three times before he got out of range."

## MYSTERIOUS LOSS

The normal tour length for RAF pilots was 100 missions and to ensure that he was back in Britain for the coronation of the new Queen, Graham Hulse decided against extending his tour. At around 1300hrs on 13 March Sqn Ldr Hulse took off in F-86E 52-2879 leading a patrol on his 95th mission. Forty minutes later as they approached the Yalu the four Sabres spotted a formation of up to 16 enemy MiGs into which he led his formation.

Selecting the leading MiG-15 Hulse closed from behind and opened fire, scoring numerous hits. The MiG began smoking profusely and decelerated, likely due to engine damage. Probably believing the fighter doomed, Hulse passed to its right before making a sharp left turn directly in front of the MiG at a very close range. The MiG pilot then fired his 37mm cannon, blowing several feet off the Sabre's left wing just as Hulse's wingman, Maj Gene Sommerich, had started firing. He hit the stricken MiG with several bursts and burning fiercely, it went into a spin and crashed near Ch'olsan. The pair were credited with its destruction. It is uncertain who the opponents were, but engagements with Soviet pilots had been made earlier in the day and most likely Hulse's formation had encountered MiGs of the Chinese 43rd Fighter Regiment. Its leader Song Ge-xiu was killed in a dogfight at this time and from a report submitted by his wingman he was also credited with shooting down a Sabre.

On his fateful final mission Hulse's wingman was Maj Gene Sommerich who finished off the MiG that had damaged his leader's Sabre. (R. Windoffer via W. Thompson)

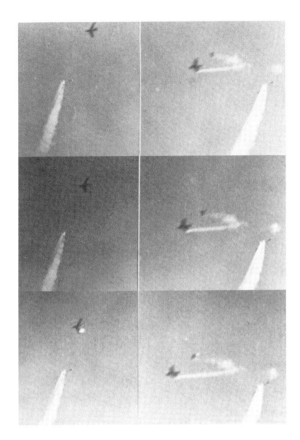

With much of his left wing shot away, Graham Hulse was seen to eject over the Ch'olsan peninsula. He was reportedly sighted on the ground several days later and a helicopter rescue mission flew to the area but sighted nothing before withdrawing under heavy fire. Sqn Ldr Graham Hulse never returned so his ultimate fate is unknown and he remains 'missing in action'. His official air combat score is one and two shared destroyed, two probable and five damaged. However, his actual total stands at three and three shared destroyed, one probable and six damaged very much making him 'the ace that never was'.

# MAU MAU
# 12 March 1954

In the east African colony of Kenya following a series of attacks on white famers and their workers a state of emergency was declared in October 1952. The extremist Kikuyu terrorist group the Mau Mau instigated an increasing number of attacks from its strongholds in the highlands of the Aberdare Range and around Mount Kenya north of the capital Nairobi. As atrocities increased, in November 1953 the first detachment of six Bomber Command Lincolns was sent out to conduct area bombing of terrorist strongholds. Led by Sqn Ldr Andrew Huchala, who was on an exchange tour from the RCAF, 61 Squadron provided the third Lincoln detachment arriving at Eastleigh, Nairobi, on 8 March 1954, to replace 100 Squadron. As well as planned attacks, two Lincolns were usually maintained on standby on the ground. To avoid the cloud build-up and resulting turbulence, the Lincolns usually operated at night or in the early morning and most daylight attacks were marked by light aircraft.

The squadron began operations on 12 March when at 1030hrs the CO left Eastleigh in RE297, one of his crew telling a journalist after landing:

> "The crew could feel the blast of their 'stick' as they swept over the Aberdares at 2,500 feet above the crest. The bombs tore a huge crater in the ground. We felt the blast and saw trees fold on themselves."

The CO was followed by the crews of Flt Lt Lang in RF555 and Sgt Myers in RE411 who took off at lunchtime. Most sorties lasted about one and a half hours. Similar numbers of sorties were flown on the succeeding days and at 2100hrs on the 18th Sgt Myers flew the first night-bombing sortie of the detachment. Sadly, when returning from a night attack in the Aberdare Range on 22 March Lincoln RE297 crashed into Mount Kinangop with the loss of Flt Lt Michael Waite and his crew of Fg Offs Michael Owen and Robbie Robinson, M/Eng Bill Beesley DFM and Sgt Jim Atkinson. Five search sorties were flown the next day to try to locate the wreckage that was not found until three days later by an infantry patrol.

Flt Lt Lang flies Lincoln B 2 RF555 over the forests around Mount Kenya during 61 Squadron's first day of anti-Mau Mau bombing attacks on 12 March 1954. (MoD)

By the end of March 61 Squadron's Lincolns had flown 46 bombing attacks in a good start to the detachment. The bomb load usually comprised up to five 1,000lb and nine 500lb bombs that were dropped from low or medium level. The stick length varied

A shortage of bombs meant supplies had to be collected from Aden such as when Sgt Grey flew Lincoln B 2 RE296 to Khormaksar on 26 May. (R. B. Trevitt)

depending on the required time of saturation. When required 350lb fragmentation bombs were also dropped. On occasion the bombers descended to low level to strafe the target with .50in machine-gun fire and bomb fuses were also set to allow for low-level attack. A journalist that flew on one low-level sortie described it as "a bit tight and somewhat hair-raising".

To separate the activity by the Mau Mau terrorists from town-based supporters to its strongholds in the Aberdare mountains and Mount Kenya between 24 April and 7 May the British-led security forces began Operation Anvil for which a detachment of Vampire jets supplemented the Lincolns. In April the Lincolns also began flying some photo-reconnaissance sorties.

A typical sortie to hit Mau Mau hideouts in the Aberdare Range would leave Eastleigh and land back three hours later. There was often a shortage of bombs so on occasion the Lincolns had to fly up to RAF Khormaksar in Aden to collect additional weapons. Lack of timely and accurate intelligence meant bombing was rather haphazard, but almost 900 insurgents had been killed or wounded by air attacks by June 1954. The bombing certainly disrupted the Mau Mau infrastructure and created difficulties for them in pursuing their terror campaign.

On 6 June a detachment from 214 Squadron arrived at Eastleigh to take over. No. 61 Squadron flew its final bombing sorties on 14 June with Flt Sgt Coulson being the last to land at 1840hrs. In a successful and busy detachment, 61 Squadron's crews had flown 159 bombing and 41 photographic sorties to make an even total of 200.

# MOMENT OF TRUTH
# 5 November 1956

Embarked in HMS *Eagle* for operations at Suez was Lt Cdr Vyvyan Howard's 830 Squadron which unlike the other strike squadrons embarked was not jet powered. It flew the unconventional Westland Wyvern S4 powered by a 4,110hp Armstrong Siddeley Python turbo-prop engine that drove a large counter-rotating airscrew. The squadron's senior pilot was the bearded Lt Cdr Bill 'Smokey' Cowling, a colourful character who had been born in the US and joined the RAF in Canada during WW2. After serving as a flying instructor he had transferred to the Royal Navy in 1945.

No. 830 Squadron's Wyverns went into action against Egypt at 0800hrs on 1 November when six aircraft each carrying a 1,000lb bomb attacked the former Fleet Air Arm airfield at Dekhelia near Alexandria. Bill Cowling recalled: "Six Wyverns in two 'vics' attacked. We concentrated on the runway intersection with a view to stopping the MiGs getting airborne." The squadron attacked the airfield at the same time the next day when one bomb struck a hangar that was destroyed. This was then followed at midday by an attack on the main transport depot of the Egyptian army at Camp Huckstep in the western suburbs of Cairo. The attack was very successful and not one of the bombs dropped by the Wyverns fell outside the target area.

The strikes continued into 3 November, and though now it was assessed that the threat from Egyptian MiGs fighters was negligible, anti-aircraft fire was a constant menace. With the EAF effectively neutralised, attacks switched to communications targets and 830 selected the El Gamil bridge west of Port Said. Although only near misses could be claimed, the bridge foundations were damaged. However, Lt Denis McCarthy's Wyvern WN330/J 379 was hit in

Lt Cdr Bill 'Smokey' Cowling. (W. H. Cowling)

A quartet of bomb-laden Wyvern S4s of 830 Squadron move forward prior to launching for a strike over Egypt. (Royal Navy)

the engine by ground fire and he steered his crippled aircraft out to sea covered by the rest of the formation until he was forced to eject near the carrier; he was soon picked up by a rescue helicopter from *Eagle*. Undaunted, six Wyverns returned later in the morning conducting a low-level attack that scored one hit on the structure. A further attack by four Wyverns shortly after 1500hrs further damaged the bridge so that by the end of the day the western end had been destroyed. After three days of intensive action the ship withdrew to refuel and embark two replacement Wyverns.

As airborne troops landed in Egypt early on 5 November 830 Squadron's Wyverns provided 'cab rank' patrols over the drop zones at El Gamil and Port Said on call to immediately neutralise any threats. Shortly after 0700hrs, five aircraft made bomb and rocket attacks onto Egyptian army positions that were repeated three hours later when a strongpoint was demolished by bombing; mortar positions in a local cemetery were also neutralised. The cover patrols continued into the afternoon and at 1440hrs Lt Cdr Cowling led another strike on the troublesome coastguard barracks. As rockets had proved ineffective, he went in low and successfully 'lobbed a 500 pounder through the window'. However, the small-arms fire was intense as Bill Cowling later described:

"I was hit by small calibre stuff but was not aware until pulling away. Funny noises – like impellor blades disappearing out of the jet pipe. The engine went into the 'red' and I decided to get as much height as possible and get away from the land. In the event I got up to 1,200 feet and had to throttle back as all the indications were that the engine was about to break up. I started screaming Mayday. The carrier acknowledged. So did Jim Summerlee who was the rescue helicopter pilot. I pulled down the face-blind which activates the explosive under the seat. I ejected about five miles off the coast of Port Said. Everything worked perfectly."

With remarkable coolness, Bill Cowling had ordered his wingman, Sub-Lt 'Scottie' Scott to photograph the ejection and record his 'moment of truth'.

Lt Cdr Summerlee in the Whirlwind was already on the scene and soon picked up his dripping colleague from the Mediterranean. Summerlee and Cowling were colleagues from a previous squadron and they celebrated his safe return later that evening. During the day 830 Squadron had dropped 17 bombs, fired 176 rockets and expended over 2,000 rounds of cannon ammunition.

The moment of truth. Lt Cdr Bill Cowling rides up the rail as he ejects from Wyvern S4 WN378 over the Mediterranean on 5 November. (W. H. Cowling)

# CYPRUS MARE'S NEST
# 9 January 1959

In Cyprus during the late 1950s British forces conducted a counter-insurgency campaign against the Greek-Cypriot guerrilla organisation known as EOKA (Ethniki Organosis Kypriou Agonistou or National Organisation of Cypriot Fighters) that aspired to a union with Greece. Among the air reinforcements sent out in late 1958 were the Scottish Aviation Pioneer CC.1 light transports of 230 Squadron under Sqn Ldr W. J. Simpson. They were to support operations by ground forces in the very difficult wooded and mountainous terrain of the Troodos and Kyrenia mountains.

The first operational sortie was flown on 1 December when Flt Lt Ted Douglas flew some casualties from Nicosia for treatment at the RAF Hospital at Akrotiri. The security forces director of operations then requested that 230 Squadron be proficient

Armed and dangerous! Flt Lts Red Hampton, Ted Douglas, Roy Burgess and Mick Lloyd who all participated in Operation Mare's Nest. (230 Squadron Records)

in the supply-dropping role, so training began using harness packs free dropped from out of the door.

Operations Mare's Nest that began on 6 January was a major internal security forces operation by 3 Brigade to clear EOKA pockets to the south of Xeros in the Troodos mountains. Before the operation began the CO had flown the COs of the participating units, the Royal Horse Guards, Grenadier Guards, Lancashire Fusiliers, Welch Regiment, Black Watch and the Parachute Regiment, over the area on an extensive reconnaissance of the rugged terrain. The cloud, rain and snow then arrived.

The local *Cyprus Mail* offered a vivid description of the conditions at the start of Op Mare's Nest:

> "In thick mud, with teeming incessant rain and a temperature not much above freezing point, British troops pressed on yesterday with their large-scale operation in the northern Troodos region. In the mid-morning downpour patrols of soldiers searched the wooded slopes. Horses and trucks entering the cordon area were stopped and questioned by Greek-speaking soldiers."

With the heavy rain washing away many of the mountain roads, after the army had lost a driver over the edge of one road in the slippery conditions, 230 Squadron's Pioneers were for the first time requested to conduct supply drops to troops engaged

Flt Lt Red Hampton climbs into Pioneer XL702 at Nicosia for a supply drop on 9 January. (230 Squadron Records)

on the ground. Flt Lt Len Sandbach therefore flew a ground liaison officer (GLO) to locate suitable drop zones (DZs) and the CO landed at Xeros to confirm the details with the Brigade HQ. After overcoming some initial resistance from the Air HQ, Flt Lt Sandbach made the first live drop on the 9th with Flt Lt Red Hampton flying another in XL702 later in the day.

Each load comprised ten 45lb packs and in all 114 drops were made onto DZs over the next ten days in very difficult country and in very poor weather that tested the pilots' skill to the full. Despite the difficulties some very good results were achieved and almost three tons of supplies were dropped. The CO wrote at the time:

"Supply dropping was considered the highlight of the Cyprus detachment. Working directly with the army in the field gave the squadron a sense of direct participation in operations. The only dissatisfied customer was a Grenadier Guardsman who foolishly strayed into the undershoot of a DZ and received a personal ration delivery in the shape of a 45lb pack. He was a sad and sorry guardsman for a few days."

Speaking of the operation at a press conference at his HQ at Xeros the commander of 3 Brigade, Brig Tony Read said:

"The operation which involves about one thousand troops covers an indefinite area over about 600 square miles and is always moving. New techniques are in the process of being tried out [referring to 230's resupply task] and old ones refined. We are patrolling very wide and in difficult country. The chief transport is feet, vehicles, helicopters and fixed-wing aircraft and a great deal of progress has been made in ground-to-air co-operation in the Cyprus hills."

A journalist noted that even as he spoke 'a Pioneer aircraft roared overhead on its way to drop supplies to isolated troops'.

Operation Mare's Nest was concluded on the 19th with a number of significant arrests and was deemed a success due in no small part to the airborne resupply provided the 230 Squadron's Pioneers.

Pioneer CC.1 XL558 en route to the Troodos mountains on a resupply sortie during Operation Mare's Nest. (230 Squadron Records)

# IRA MANHUNT
## 3 April 1960

In December 1956, the Irish Republican Army (IRA) began a campaign of bombing and shooting incidents along the border with the republic and the British province of Northern Ireland. The terrorists usually targeted customs posts, police stations and 'loyalist' assembly buildings. By 1959 it was evident that to counter the upsurge in violence that the Royal Ulster Constabulary (RUC), would benefit from some form of air mobility. Thus, on 1 September 1959, 118 Squadron was reformed at Aldergrove with three Bristol Sycamore HR14 helicopters (XE317, XG506, and XG521) tasked to support the army and RUC in anti-IRA operations:

(a) reconnaissance;
(b) cordon and search working with the army and the police on the ground;
(c) rapid air transport of small parties of soldiers/police in the operational role.

The squadron few its first internal security operation on 11 September and soon afterwards Sqn Ldr David Toon arrived as the CO. He recalled:

Parked at Aldergrove both Sycamore HR14s XG506 and XG521 were used on the cordon and search operation for the terrorists in the Belleek area. (D. A. Toon)

"The border with the Republic was closed apart from some key crossing points and it was surprising how easy it was to spot illegal crossings at first light when footprints showed up clearly in the morning dew – which was invariably heavy in Northern Ireland!"

The IRA were active and on 12 February 1960 Toon's helicopter came under machine-gun fire during an operation near Magherafelt, but without damage.

During the night of 3 April, a group of IRA terrorists ambushed an RUC patrol near Belleek in Co. Fermanagh about 25 miles west of Enniskillen. Belleek straddles the border and is the most westerly village in the United Kingdom.

Flt Lt Mike Taylor (right) and Fg Off Gordon Lear flew a cordon and search operation on 4 April. (F. M. Taylor)

Following the ambush the IRA group then attempted to evade the extensive follow-up search that had begun and presumably to try to escape across the nearby border. At 0400hrs the standby helicopter was called out and flown by Fg Off Bob Martin with M/Nav R. W. Chambers and LAC B. Jenkins as crewman it left Aldergrove at 0545hrs.

Sqn Ldr David Toon (second from right) with RUC Special Branch at Belleek before getting airborne in Sycamore HR14 XG521 to control the search for the IRA group on 5 April. (D. A. Toon)

Heavily armed RUC policemen strap into Sqn Ldr Toon's Sycamore before being dropped off during the search for the IRA ambush party. (D. A. Toon)

The crew flew to Belleek where Martin was briefed by the police commander before conducting an extensive reconnaissance of the area where the terrorists were thought to be. Great care had to be taken not to cross the border. The aircraft then returned to Aldergrove where they learned that the RUC had reported that the helicopter's presence overhead had kept the IRA men pinned down so preventing them from leaving the area and crossing back over the border. The police operation continued, but the terrorists had apparently gone to ground.

The following afternoon two Sycamores flown by Flt Lt Mike Taylor in XG506 with his navigator Fg Off Gordon Lear and Fg Off Martin and M/Nav Chalmers in XG521 flew down to support an RUC cordon and search operation in the Aughanduff mountains west of Newry, Co. Armagh. Each crew flew several troop lifts dropping nine policemen before returning to base.

Early the following morning, 5 April, came a further request for air support from the RUC that were still hunting the IRA group that had conducted the ambush at Belleek. During the night there had been reports that the men who were armed with Thompson sub-machine guns were terrorising local inhabitants, demanding food and shelter. At 0525hrs Sqn Ldr Toon in XG521 with M/Nav Chambers and Flt Sgt Spinks with M/Nav Hall in XE317 took off in poor weather and headed for Belleek. On arrival, the CO was briefed by officers of the RUC Special Branch before both aircraft began dropping police sections to form a cordon. Later each crew flew two recces around the area while an RUC officer on board David Toon's aircraft, in radio contact with the ground, controlled the search. This culminated in complete success when the IRA suspects were arrested and a quantity of arms and ammunition seized.

# LAST MAN OUT
## 21 April 1975

The withdrawal of most US and Allied combat forces resulted in the Communist North Vietnamese forces launching several large-scale offensives against South Vietnam from December 1974. On 4 March 1975 over 300,000 North Vietnamese regular troops opened the Ho Chi Minh Campaign in the Central Highlands. The capture of the cities of Quảng Trị, Hué and Da Nang before the end of the month provoked near panic in the South Vietnamese forces. The Communist commander, Gen Văn Tiến Dũng, had said that he would 'liberate' Saigon before the rainy season that began in mid-May. By 1 April South Vietnam began to implode resulting in evacuation plans being implemented by its former Allies.

At the beginning of April the New Zealand ambassador Norman Farrell cabled Wellington recommending the immediate withdrawal of all non-essential New Zealand personnel. The evacuation task was given to 41 Squadron RNZAF based at Tengah, Singapore under Sqn Ldr Bob Davidson who then led a detachment to Saigon's main airport at Tan Son Nhut. On 4 April three elderly Bristol Freighters,

All three RNZAF Freighters, NZ5903, NZ5904 and NZ5907 at Tan Son Nhut on 8 April.
(Sqn Ldr R. Davidson via P. Tremayne)

The 41 Squadron accommodation was fortified with bags of rice and thus christened 'the Rice Redoubt'. (Sqn Ldr R. Davidson via P. Tremayne)

NZ5903 flown by Flt Lt Denis Monti, NZ5904 (Sqn Ldr Roger Holdaway) and NZ5907 (Flt Lt Don Carter) flew to Saigon carrying stores and some ground crew. Two aircraft then returned to Tengah with some evacuees leaving Freighter NZ5907 in South Vietnam. This aircraft flew the first evacuation flight that night to lift out the New Zealand Services Medical Team from Quy Nhon 250 miles to the north-east. The next day the North Vietnamese captured Nha Trang when Sqn Ldr Holdaway's crew flew two trips each carrying 4,000lb of rice to An Thoi on Phu Quoc island off the coast to which over 60,000 South Vietnamese refugees had escaped.

Regular shuttle flights between Singapore and Saigon also began as well as to country locations, where there were now desperate food shortages. At Tan Son Nhut the Kiwis set up camp with an HQ, ops room and accommodation alongside the control tower where it was fortified with bags of rice. This resulted in it soon being dubbed as the Rice Redoubt. On 8 April Flt Lt Carter's crew in Freighter NZ5904 flew relief supplies into the former Australian base at Vũng Tàu though the aircraft landed in the face of intense small-arms fire from Viet Cong guerrillas. The following day the Battle of Xuân Lộc, just 50 miles east of the capital, began resulting in the situation in Saigon rapidly deteriorating.

Bristol Freighter NZ5903 delivering relief supplies to refugees at An Thoi on Phú Quốc Island on 7 April 1975. The crew are from left to right: Flt Lt Denis Monti, Sqn Ldr Roger Barson, Flt Sgt Bob Brumfitt, and Sqn Ldr Pete White. (Sqn Ldr R. Davidson via P. Tremayne)

Flt Lt Don Carter in NZ5904 flew the last in-country relief flight to An Thoi, on 12 April as these were then halted due to the increased risks. This aircraft flown by Sqn Ldr Holdaway then returned to Tengah with spare aircrew and some servicing personnel. Then on 20 April Flt Lt Monti flew the final round trip when in NZ5903 he flew in a load of milk powder and returned with further ground crew and more evacuees.

Remaining at Tan Son Nhut with Freighter NZ5907 was Sqn Ldr Davidson and his crew who was under the strict orders that he was not to withdraw the detachment without the embassy staff along with any other remaining New Zealand nationals.

Xuân Lộc, the last major battle of the long Vietnam War, ended on 21 April. This then put Tan Son Nhut within range of North Vietnamese artillery so Mr Farrell the ambassador therefore ordered the evacuation of his staff and the last New Zealand nationals. These last New Zealanders, including Norman Farrell, made their way to Tan Son Nhut where they embarked on Bristol Freighter NZ5907 captained by Flt Lt Don Carter with Fg Off Richards, Sqn Ldr Peter White and the CO as crew. During a tense afternoon the crew and their 33 passengers sat in the aircraft

Last man out. Mr Norman Farrell, the New Zealand ambassador, with his staff takes his leave of Saigon in Freighter NZ5907 ahead of the advancing Communists on 21 April. (Sqn Ldr R. Davidson via P. Tremayne)

awaiting departure clearance which after a nervous and seemingly interminable period eventually came through. Don Carter then started engines, taxied out and gratefully lifted the laden and vulnerable Freighter off Tan Son Nhut's runway and headed for Singapore with 'the last man out'. The Freighter's departure brought to an end New Zealand's involvement in the Vietnam War.

The assault on Saigon began soon afterwards and Communist tanks entered the city on 30 April.

# BLUFF COVE
# 8 June 1982

After the outbreak of war following the Argentinian invasion of the Falkland Islands in April 1982, 825 Naval Air Squadron was reformed at RNAS Culdrose under Lt Cdr H. S. Clark on 7 May. Its Sea King HAS.2 anti-submarine helicopters had their sonar equipment removed and they were modified for the troop-carrying role to supplement the dedicated commando helicopters. After a rapid work-up the unit sailed south on the liner *Queen Elizabeth 2* and container ship *Atlantic Causeway* a week later. The first elements of 825 Squadron went ashore to the forward operating base at San Carlos on 29 May beginning operations immediately.

Due to the reduced number of helicopters following the loss of the SS *Atlantic Conveyer*, ships were required to move elements of 5 Infantry Brigade forward as the British forces advanced on Port Stanley. Thus, early on 8 June the landing ships RFA *Sir Tristam*

Lt Cdr Hugh Clark was the CO of 825 Squadron who led the helicopter rescue efforts. (Royal Navy)

and RFA *Sir Galahad* anchored at Port Pleasant in Bluff Cove on East Falkland and they began offloading. The activity was seen by Argentinian observers situated on high ground above the cove and who reported the landings, information that was transmitted back to mainland Argentina. At 1400hrs the ships came under attack by seven A-4B Skyhawks of 5 Grupo de Caza that made a devastating strike hitting both ships. *Sir Galahad* was struck by three bombs dropped by 1°Lt Carlos Cachón resulting in a devastating fire.

With a Sea King hovering alongside, the RFA *Sir Galahad* burns fiercely at anchor in Bluff Cove. (Royal Navy)

Earlier, Lt Cdr Clark had landed a survey party at nearby Fitzroy and once the attack was over with his co-pilot Sub-Lt Brian Evans and crewman CPO David Jackson got airborne in Sea King HAS.2 XV700. Almost immediately they were presented with an apocalyptic sight. *Sir Galahad* was already a blazing inferno billowing thick black oily smoke with the water around it already filled with life rafts and men in life vests. Three more aircraft of his squadron flown by Lts Phil Sheldon flying XV654, John Boughton (in XV663) and Steve Isacke in XZ580 also arrived and began recovering survivors from the water and direct from the shattered ships. Many of the men picked up had dreadful burns and most were suffering from shock. They were flown ashore where first-aid stations had been set up before the crews returned to the blazing scene.

Lt Cdr Hugh Clark's Sea King edges closer to the blazing landing ship *Sir Galahad* to rescue survivors after the devastating Argentine air attack at Bluff Cove on 8 June 1982. (Royal Navy)

The Sea Kings flown by Boughton and Sheldon picked up men, many of whom were injured or in shock, from the confined area of the ship's foredeck where the proximity of masts and rigging left little clearance for the aircraft which were often covered by the acrid and blinding smoke. Nonetheless, they continued even as ammunition and fuel were exploding. Evacuation and rescue work was maintained until interrupted by another Argentinian air attack.

In some of the most dramatic images of the campaign that were later flashed around the world Hugh Clark hovered his aircraft in the blinding acrid smoke as survivors were lifted into the aircraft. Then seeing other injured men trapped in the congested area of the burning deck, he also eased the aircraft over the deck to winch them to safety. In a most remarkable episode of imagination and clear thinking, Hugh Clark, soon followed by others, then carefully manoeuvred his helicopter low over the water so that the downwash from its rotors helped 'push' the life rafts away from the blazing ship toward the safety of the shoreline. Once the immediate rescue was completed the four 825 Squadron crews then began ferrying the casualties to the field hospital at Ajax Bay, a task that continued deep into the night.

Bluff Cove was the worst single action of the war that left 56 men dead and 150 injured but that also saw some of the highest acts of gallantry. There was no respite and the Sea Kings of 825 Squadron continued to support the advance on Stanley, including lifting men, artillery and stores to the forward positions until the Argentinian

Two 825 Squadron Sea Kings close on the bow of *Sir Galahad* to lift off survivors. (Royal Navy)

Both Lts Phil Sheldon (left) and John Boughton (right) were decorated for their actions at Bluff Cove. (Royal Navy)

surrender on 14 June. An indication of how busy this period was is shown that when supporting the Welsh Guards and Gurkhas during the final advance, Lt Cdr Robin Everall flew over ten hours during the day.

In mid-July the squadron sailed home in *Atlantic Causeway*, flying off to Culdrose on the 27th and where it was disbanded on 17 September. For their actions at Bluff Cove, Lt Cdr Hugh Clark was awarded the DSC while Lts John Boughton and Phil Sheldon each received the QGM.

# AMBUSH OVER ANGOLA
## 30 September 1985

Throughout the 1970s and 1980s the SAAF was constantly in action over Angola and South-West Africa (Namibia) supporting cross-border attacks against terrorist bases to counter incursions by the SWAPO liberation movement. By the mid-1980s whilst operating over parts of southern Angola, the SAAF was facing some of the heaviest air defences anywhere in the world manned by Cuban and Soviet 'volunteers'. The Angolans were also increasingly using helicopters for resupply and support, which was a critical element in the wild bush that had few roads or other easy means of transport where pro-Western UNITA guerrillas made road movement dangerous.

In a bid to halt helicopter re-supply to the forward areas, in early September 1985 during the Angolan push towards the UNITA stronghold at Mavinga the SAAF devised an operation to interdict the helicopters. Eighteen Impala IIs (Macchi MB-326K) drawn from 4 and 8 Squadrons were re-positioned to the forward airfield at Rundu in the Kavango region that lies on the Okavango river. Rundu was 3,000ft above sea level and located right on the Angolan border. Their aim was to mount regular

A 4 Squadron Impala II taxiing out at the time the SAAF set up its cleverly devised ambush of the Angolan helicopters. (D. Van Rensburg)

Eleven of the 18 Impalas of 4 and 8 Squadrons at Rundu in September 1985 for the anti-helicopter operation. (L. Reid)

anti-helicopter combat air patrols over the Lomba river area to destroy this Angolan capability. South African special forces patrols had established observation positions (OP) near the Angolan helicopter base at Cuito Cuanavale from which they could monitor the movement of Angolan helicopters. The patrol would then radio in to their HQ to scramble the Impalas every time the helicopters took off. The Impalas would then run their CAP over the Lomba river in an attempt to visually detect the helicopters.

The initial scrambles proved abortive, but a scramble in the late afternoon of 27 September brought success. Capt Leon Maré flying Impala 1054 leading Capt Pine Pienaar (of 8 Squadron) in 1057 were scrambled on being notified of a pair of helicopters setting out. Some 30 minutes after launching Pienaar spotted a pair of Mil Mi-25 'Hind D' gunship helicopters, one of which was No. H-322 being flown by an Angolan pilot. Being in a favourable position Capt Pienaar climbed above the rear Mi-25 and attacked, as he later recalled:

"I aimed slightly above my chopper and pulled the trigger, firing for what seemed an awfully long time. There were bright flashes, followed by an audible *whooff* and the chopper started burning from underneath. The flames stopped, replaced by brown smoke."

The helicopter started to dive in a controlled descent firing off its rockets and jettisoning other stores. In the meantime, Maré attacked the second helicopter that began a steep descent as he made a quarter astern attack from below. As the helicopter turned through 180 degrees he opened fire hitting the fuselage below the main rotor gearbox. The Hind's nose suddenly dropped and as the rotor blades separated the Hind crashed to the ground and exploded. Pienaar meanwhile had repositioned to make a second attack on his target:

"Both pilots were clearly visible and very busy fighting to remain airborne. There was a sparkling ripple of hits along the cowling, the high-explosive shells tearing apart engines, drive shaft and gearbox. The helicopter rolled violently onto its left side, blades folding into a tangled mess and I knew this particular Mi-25 was going nowhere but down."

As the rotor blades detached the Hind fell away and exploded on impact. The two Impalas then egressed at low level back to Rundu.

The success was repeated on 30 September when six Impalas scrambled to fly three combat air patrols over the likely routes. The first section comprised Cmdt Andre 'Neefie' van den Heever, OC 4 Squadron in Impala 1091 and Capt Wayne Westoby in 1046. They intercepted a formation of four helicopters comprising two Mi-17 'Hips' and two Mi-25s from Cuito Cuanavale flying their usual route towards the battle zone, one of the latter being flown by Ten Didi Panguila. There was also a MiG patrol reported in the area at higher level as well as some Su-22s flying a diversionary strike. Wayne Westoby recalled:

"I saw four helicopters flying east to west following the Lomba river. Two Mi-17s were in front with two Mi-25s behind them, all were flying in a trail spaced about 300 metres from each other, except for the last Mi-25 which lagged the rest by about 1,000 metres. When I called the choppers visual Andre called for a turn hard left and instructed me to lead the attack. I positioned myself so that the rearmost chopper was above me in my one o'clock.

"I began my pitch up to about 3,000ft, the Impala is quite underpowered and so the energy bled off fast. I had an almost uncontrollable nervous shake, more scared of failure than anything else. The stadiametric ranging on our gun sights was set for the chopper's main rotor blade diameter and a firing range of 250 metres. When about 400–500ft below the Mi-25, I started firing at a range of 300 metres. Nothing happened. Just as the realisation started to sink in that I had missed, the chopper exploded into a fireball."

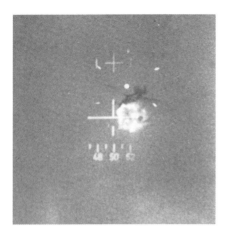

Capt Westoby's cannon fire explodes on the Mi-25 'Hind D' flown by Ten Didi Panguila on 30 September and is clearly seen in the Impala's gunsight. (W. Westoby)

However, the long firing burst had caused his engine to flame out, so he rapidly attempted a relight. His section leader Cmdt van den Heever, went for the other Mi-24 as he described:

"I pitched up to a position higher and eight o'clock to the next Mi-25. I fired at approximately 500 metres and saw the rear part of the tail boom coming off, it passed to my right and slightly below. I broke to the right and shifted my attention to the two Mi-17s which were now in a steep descent. Wayne was passing below and to the left of me, tracking one of the Mi-17s."

Having been warned by a radio call from Panguila, the two Mi-17s were aware that something had happened behind them and the rear Hip evaded frantically as Westoby, having successfully relit his engine attacked:

An Angolan Mi-17 'Hip' desperately tries to evade as the Impala flown by Capt Westoby closes on it over the Lomba river during the second successful intercept sortie. (W. Westoby)

"One of the Mi-17s up front had started a right turn towards the north. I pitched up and behind him so that I was above him in about his four or five o'clock, and fired a burst that hit him in the gearbox. He rolled to the right until inverted and went down remaining so until impacting the ground."

The second pair of Impalas then joined in. Lt Kevin Truter and wingman Lt Dudley Trollip attacked the remaining Mi-17 flown by Ten Fernando Manuel. It began zigzagging to evade Truter's attack as Trollip described:

"I observed the tail boom breaking off as they touched down. Kevin called the pitch and I stayed low to look for missile launches. He rolled in and I saw his 30mm burst scoring a direct hit, a dark orange ball of flame erupting from the mid-section of the chopper."

The pilots and some passengers survived.

Warned by a two-seat Impala flying as communications relay, the four Impalas then avoided the MiG patrol and returned to base in triumph. It had been a remarkable few days for the SAAF that at a stroke had neutralised a massive enemy capability and deterred its use in the operational area.

The unexplained loss of six helicopters stunned the Communists as they had no reason of the cause. As a cover, the

The four 4 Squadron's 'Hip Hunters' at Rundu. Rear from left to right: Capt Leon Maré and Cmdt Andre van den Heever. Front from left to right: Lt Kevin Truter and Capt Wayne Westoby. (W. Westoby)

South Africans agreed UNITA should claim that it shot down six Angolan helicopters using shoulder-launched MANPAD missiles. Soviet-flown Mi-17s evacuated Soviet advisors to the Angolan army on the night of 5 October under cover of two MiGs flown by Lt Col Sergei Sergeyevich Kriviets and Maj Valeri Panteleimonovich Nierchu. Angolan helicopter operations were suspended soon afterwards and provided no support as the Angolan brigades began their retreat from Mavinga. The message was clear, the Angolan troops were dispensable, but their Soviet advisors were not.

The SAAF had brilliantly achieved its aim.

# PATROL BOAT ATTACK
# 30 January 1991

As part of the international response to the Iraqi invasion of Kuwait on 2 August 1990 the Canadian government deployed two squadrons with an eventual total of 24 CF-18A Hornet fighters to the Gulf region. After working-up the Canadian CF-18 operations were fully integrated into coalition air defence activity to deter further Iraqi aggression. Based at Doha in Qatar, in mid-December 439 Squadron under Lt Col Don Matthews with Maj Russ Cooper as his deputy arrived from Bad Solingen in Germany as the framework unit, being supplemented by 416 Squadron from Cold Lake in Canada; they were nicknamed 'The Desert Cats'. The squadron provided combat air patrols (CAPs) to cover Allied warships from Iraqi attack and were totally integrated with the largely US Navy air umbrella. The Canadian unit flew 18 sorties per day with most refuelling from a Canadian or Allied tanker.

When Operation Desert Storm opened with a devastating air campaign on the night of 16 January 1991 439 Squadron was fully operational with all aircraft armed with three AIM-7 Sparrow and four AIM-9M Sidewinder missiles and the integral 20mm cannon. In addition to providing CAPs, 439 Squadron was tasked with sweep

Carrying Sparrow missiles underwing and Sidewinders on the wingtips, a CF-18A Hornet of 439 Squadron refuels during a CAP over the northern Gulf in January 1991. (DND/RCAF)

Ground crew load an AIM-7 Sparrow onto a Hornet, one of which was fired at the Iraqi fast patrol boat. (DND/RCAF)

and escort to sanitise the airspace ahead of strike packages flying deep into Iraq and Kuwait. The first raids covered by 439 Squadron were on the 24th covering RAF Tornados and Buccaneers though their main 'customers' were the Doha-based F-16s of the US 401st Tactical Fighter Wing (TFW). During one escort to a package of USAF F-16s from the 401st TFW, Maj Bill Ryan called the smoke of a pair of surface-to-air missiles that streaked towards the formation but that fortunately fell short. On three occasions the 439 Squadron Hornets on CAP were vectored towards inbound hostile 'tracks' but on each occasion the intruders turned away before engagement.

Following intelligence of possible Iraqi air attacks on shipping in the Gulf the squadron's CAP commitment was increased though it was against a surface threat that provided 439 Squadron with its first taste of action.

Whilst on CAP at 0200hrs on 30 January Maj David Kendall and Capt Steve Hill were directed by the on-station E-2C Hawkeye to fill a gap in armed surface reconnaissance. A US Navy A-6E Intruder had located four Iraqi TNC-45 fast patrol boats equipped with Exocet anti-ship missiles and were a high threat to Allied ships. The A-6 crew had engaged three of the Iraqi warships before it expended its weapons and the two Hornets were then vectored to engage the fourth vessel.

Maj David Kendall (left) and Capt Steve Hill of 439 Squadron after their engagement with the Iraqi patrol boat. The ground crew have already applied a 'kill' marking. (DND/RCAF)

As they approached they sighted the speeding fast patrol boat that was clearly illuminated in the bright moonlight. Despite the threat from its anti-aircraft guns, both the CF-18s made strafing passes with hits from the 20mm cannon fire observed. Kendall and Hill then made several passes in attempts to obtain a weapons system lock for the air-to-ground mode on the Sidewinder missiles. However, the heat signature from the FPB's engines was insufficient to obtain a lock. In a subsequent pass, Maj Kendall using the APG-65 radar obtained a full system lock on air-to-air mode and launched a Sparrow missile which impacted the water close to the boat. As a result of this proximity explosion and by hits from the cannon fire irreparable damage was caused and the boat's destruction was completed by a US aircraft. The Canadian pilots were credited with a half share in the patrol boat's demise.

This was the combat debut for the CF-18 and also the first occasion of Canadian pilots opening fire in combat since the Korean War 40 years earlier. The 439 Squadron CF-18s continued flying escort and CAPs and later began flying ground-attack sorties, making 56 bombing sorties against Iraqi forces until Kuwait was liberated and a ceasefire declared on 28 February.

# CURBING SADDAM
# 13 January 1993

Following the end of the Gulf War in March 1991 the Allied coalition continued to monitor the activities of the Iraqi regime under Saddam Hussain. As a result of the persecution of the marsh Arabs in southern Iraq a 'no-fly zone' (NFZ) south of the 32nd parallel had been imposed and to police it the Allies maintained significant air assets in the Gulf region. The British contribution was a detachment of Tornado GR1s and in late 1992 14 Squadron was the lead unit, though the aircraft came from a variety of units. Shortly after Christmas the Iraqis began one of their periodic tests of Allied resolve by moving missiles into and around the NFZ posing a threat to Allied aircraft that were policing the UN-imposed NFZ.

Several operations to curb the Iraqi deployments and to demonstrate Allied commitment were planned but then shelved. However, in early January 1993 it was decided to strike at the key nodal points of the Iraqi air defence system within the NFZ with individual operational buildings and radars being targeted. Planned for the evening of 13 January, the attack would involve some 40 US, British and French strike aircraft with a huge supporting force of tankers, AWACS and electronic warfare aircraft taking the total to over 100 aircraft.

A pair of Tornado GR1s refuelling from a Victor tanker at the time of Operation Ingleton, the nearest aircraft, ZD849/AJ-F designated for Sqn Ldr Napier's attack. (M. J. W. Napier)

With a TIAl D pod underneath, Tornado GR1 ZA479/AJ-L 617 Squadron was the spare aircraft for Op Ingleton on 13 January 1993. (M. J. W. Napier)

To the strike package the RAF would contribute four Tornado GR1s, operating in two pairs, with one airborne spare, as well as refuelling tankers. The first pair were to attack the HQ of the Integrated Operations Centre (IOC) near Musay Idah about ten miles south of Al-Amarah, on the Tigris river. The second pair of Tornados, having taken off 15 minutes later, would bomb the adjacent Al-Amarah radar control building, just 40 seconds after the first attack. The attacks were time coordinated with the other Allied elements, for example a USAF F-15E strike following them against another control building and radar aerials. In each pair of Tornados one aircraft carried a laser-designator (TIALD) pod and would mark the target with a laser to guide in the 1,000lb Paveway II laser-guided bombs (LGB) bombs dropped by the second aircraft. The RAF participation was code named Operation Ingleton.

Sqn Ldr Mike Napier with his navigator Fg Off Chris Platt of 14 Squadron in Tornado GR1 ZA492/DA led the first pair and took off from Dhahran on the east coast of Saudi Arabia before heading for their first refuelling. Sqn Ldr Napier later recalled:

"After a feint, we turned north-east to cross the Euphrates 20 miles east of Tallil, before turning again, onto our attack track of east-north-east for the run into Al-Amarah. Off the target, we would pick up a track just west of south to head directly back towards the Saudi border."

With timing critical, the first crews adjusted their speed before hitting their 'push point' and ingressed towards their target, constantly scanning the ground and the on-board sensors for signs of Iraqi gunfire or missiles. Having flown along the River Euphrates valley a change in wind meant that they had to briefly engage afterburner to adjust the timing so illuminating the aircraft. Shortly afterwards the Tornado was illuminated by an SA-2 missile fire-control radar and as the pilot manoeuvred to check for incoming missiles, the navigator activated defensive chaff.

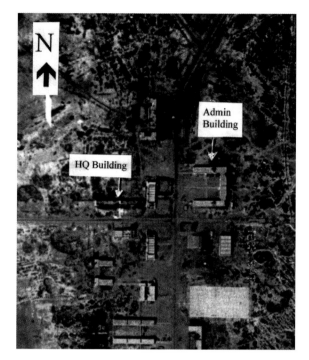

After the excitement, they ran in towards the target with a river bridge beyond the target appearing on the radar to confirm the accuracy of the weapons system. A brief radio call to the No. 2 gained confirmation that in Tornado GR1 ZD849/ AJ-F Flt Lt Mal Hudson

Left: A reconnaissance photograph of the Al-Amarah HQ of the Integrated Operations Centre (IOC) HQ building. (MoD)

Below: A Paveway II LGB explodes in the Al-Amarah HQ building during Op Ingleton. (MoD)

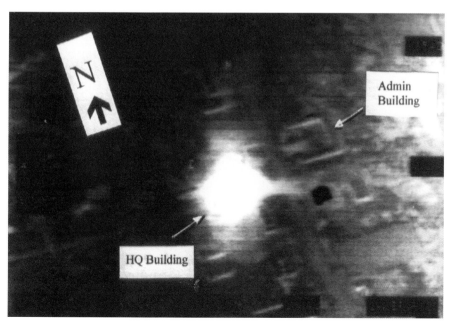

Sqn Ldr Mike Napier in front of Tornado GR1 ZA492/DA that he flew on Operation Ingleton on which the ground crew have already painted an LGB symbol under the cockpit. (M. J. W. Napier)

and his navigator Flt Lt Steve Kennedy had acquired the target on the TIALD pod and it was being illuminated ready for weapon release. With the target identified, the weapons system counted down and the three LGBs were released in turn and began guiding to the target building. Less than a minute behind, the second pair of Tornados began their final run in. After release, the four Tornados then cleared the area as Mike Napier described:

"We wheeled off to the south-east to clear the triple-A sites along the Tigris. Behind us as we turned, I was aware of a flash as the weapons exploded. Meanwhile the radio calls told me that Nos. 3 and 4 were also prosecuting their attack successfully. Some of the boys later told me that they could see muzzle flashes beneath us on the banks of the Tigris, but I saw nothing."

The return flight proved uneventful and after landing the review of the TIALD video in the Reconnaissance Intelligence Centre revealed the bombs detonating directly on target. It was the first of a number of kinetic operations mounted over the next ten years aimed at curbing Saddam's worst excesses.

# FULL CIRCLE
## 25 January 2013

In 2012, following a military coup d'état, rebel groups including Islamist militants with links to al-Qaeda began to violently take control of northern parts of the West African state of Mali. They swiftly captured Timbuktu and Gao and in January 2013, Ansar al-Din ejected the Malian army out of the city of Konna, 370 miles north-east of the capital Bamako. The various groups then affiliated as the Jama'a Nusrat ul-Islam wa al-Muslimin. Following a request for military assistance, France launched Operation Serval and the intervention began on 11 January to stop the militants advancing further south. This included air strikes near the city of Gao where two Islamist bases with fuel stocks and weapon dumps were destroyed. To enable their operations within the wide expanses of the Sahara the French requested some specialist assistance from the UK, including a 'wide area surveillance' capability. The request was approved and the latter was a role that the RAF's Sentinel R1 had successfully delivered in Afghanistan and Libya.

At Waddington planning and preparations for a deployment to West Africa by 5 Squadron under Wg Cdr Al Marshall began immediately and a Sentinel with ground

Sentinel R1 ZJ694 departs from Waddington en route to Dakar in support of French military operations in Mali on 25 January 2013. (MoD)

Sqn Ldr Setterfield (right) lines up Sentinel R1 ZJ694 for take-off at Dakar on one of the first missions on Operation Newcombe. (MoD)

support was prepared and crews briefed. A liaison team under Capt Paul Keymer was sent to the French HQ at Bamako though it was decided to base the aircraft at the French air base at Dakar in Senegal. The Sentinel was to provide reconnaissance information gathered by its dual-mode radar that comprised a synthetic aperture radar (SAR) and ground-moving target indication (GMTI). This provided a unique intelligence capability in support of the French operations within Mali. The primary mission was to cover sparsely populated parts of north and central Mali in order to track rebel units or static locations that could then be attacked by air or ground forces. The information gathered also built up a general intelligence picture as the crew were also able to capture near photographic-quality images of activity on the ground over a vast area in any weather, day or night. Analysts would then interpret the battlefield picture that helped to determine the pattern of future operations.

Under Operation Newcombe, on 25 January Sentinel ZJ694 flown by Flt Lts Swann and Darling left Waddington for Dakar where it arrived the next day. The initial priority was the collection of SAR imagery of vast swathes of northern Mali where French ground operations had begun. The 5 Squadron detachment began operations on 30 January when at 0830hrs the Sentinel flown by Sqn Ldr Chris Setterfield lifted off from Dakar and headed east. Just to get there the aircraft had to fly the equivalent of London to Rome. The crew were tasked with providing SAR and GMTI coverage in the vicinity of the towns of Tessalit, deep in the Sahara on the border with Algeria, and Kidal, 150 miles to the south. During the two and a half hours on station over northern Mali the crew took two-dozen SAR images to provide the essential intelligence requested. Using the GMTI they positively

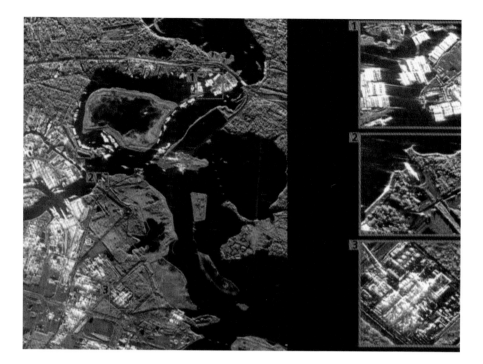

A typical synthetic aperture radar picture provided by the Sentinel over Mali. (MoD)

identified a convoy of friendly troops and also passed a 'track of interest' for investigation by a French army patrol.

The two towns were covered again the next day when additionally the village of Aguelhok that was situated on Route Nationale 19 was also covered. GMTI revealed a collection of 30 vehicles on the main supply route (MSR) and the 'product' gathered was then disseminated. After three and a half hours on task the aircraft began the three-hour flight back to Dakar. It was the start of a busy four months for the ordered detachment that was to fly six missions a week. These sorties were in support of the rapid French advance that soon saw the fall of the Tuareg MNLA stronghold at Kidal and much of northern Mali. However, in the face of French firepower the Islamists generally melted away making the Sentinel's surveillance capability even more valuable.

Another early task for the aircraft was to establish the condition of a bridge across the River Niger at Tassiga that had been reportedly blown up. This was critical information as it spanned a canyon across which UN-backed troops from Niger and Chad were to open a new front. The 5 Squadron detachment soon settled into a routine though the tropical heat and unserviceability were not the only problems encountered.

The aircraft dispersal was adjacent to a wooded area from which spitting cobra and black mamba snakes occasionally ventured, while an 18-foot-long python was found next to a French AWACS parked nearby.

With the information provided by the Sentinel, through mid-February, the French troops spread across northern Mali and, with support from Chadian forces, attacked the AQIM sanctuary in the Adrar des Ifoghas massif in the north so that by April Operation Serval had achieved its main aims. Thus on 20 May the Sentinel detachment returned to Waddington having completed 66 missions and almost 700 hours flying.

The Sentinel's mission crew monitor movement over the vast empty tracts of northern Mali looking for rebel movement. (MoD)

With an eerie symmetry, its army cooperation sorties in concert with French forces echoed those when the squadron first went to war a century earlier. No. 5 Squadron really had come full circle.

In the pre-dawn darkness at Dakar, ground crew ready a Sentinel for its next surveillance sortie over Mali. (MoD)

# SELECT BIBLIOGRAPHY

Banks, Arthur, *Wings of the Dawning: The Battle for the Indian Ocean 1939-1945*, Images Ltd., 1996

Boiten, Theo, *Bristol Blenheim*, Crowood, 1998

Boiten, Theo, *Nachtjagd Combat Archive: Vols 1–12*, Red Kite, 2018-2022

Bowyer, Chaz, *RAF Operations 1918–1939*, William Kimber, 1988

Bowyer, Michael J. F., *Fighting Colours: RAF Fighter Camouflage and Markings, 1937–1969*, Patrick Stevens, 1969/1975

Brown, James Ambrose, *Eagles Strike: The Campaigns of the SAAF in Egypt, Cyrenaica, Libya, Tunisia, Tripolitania and Madagascar 1941–1943*, Purnell, 1974

Burdon, Rodney et al, *Falklands the Air War*, Arms and Armour Press, 1986

Chhina, Sqn Ldr Rana T. S., *The Eagle Strikes: The Royal Indian Air Force 1932–1950*, United Services Institute of India, 2006

Chorley, W. R., *Royal Air Force Bomber Command Losses Vols 1–9*, Midland Publishing, 1992–2009

Claringbold, Michael, Ingman, Peter, *South Pacific Air War Vol 1-4*, Avonmore Books, 2017–2020

Cole, Christopher (Ed.), *Royal Flying Corps Communiques 1915-1916*, Tom Donovan, 1990

Cole, Christopher, *Royal Air Force Communiques 1918*, Tom Donovan, 1990

Cull, Brian, Lander, Bruce, *Twelve Days in May*, Grub Street, 1995

Cull, Brian et al, *Wings over Suez*, Grub Street, 1996

Cull, Brian, Galea, Frederick, *Marylands over Malta*, Wise Owl, 2010

Douglas, W. A. B., *The Official History of the Royal Canadian Air Force Vol. III*, University of Toronto Press, 1986

Dye, Dr Peter J. et al, *Lawrence of Arabia & Middle East Air Power*, Cross & Cockade, 2016

Flintham, Vic, *High Stakes: Britain's Air Arms in Action 1945–1990*, Pen & Sword, 2009

Flintham, Vic, Thomas, Andrew, *Combat Codes: A Full Explanation and Listing of British, Commonwealth and Allied Air Force Unit Codes Since 1938*, Airlife, 2003/2008

Franks, Norman et al, *Above the War Fronts*, Grub Street, 1997

Franks, Norman, *Fighter Command's Air War 1941*, Pen & Sword, 2016

Franks, Norman, *Forever Strong: The Story of 75 Squadron RNZAF 1916–1990*, Random Century, 1990

Franks, Norman, *RAF Fighter Command 1936-1968*, Patrick Stephens, 1992

Franks, Norman, *Royal Air Force Fighter Command Losses of the Second World War Vols 1–3*, Midland, 1997–2000

Franks, Norman, *Sharks among Minnows: Germany's First Fighter Pilots and the Fokker Eindecker Period, July 1915 to September 1916*, Grub Street, 2001

Franks, Norman, *The Greatest Air Battle: Dieppe 19th August 1942*, Grub Street, 1992

Franks, Norman et al, *The Jasta War Chronology: A Complete Listing of Claims and Losses, August 1916– November 1918*, Grub Street, 1998

Gilson, Douglas, *Royal Australian Air Force 1939–1942*, Australian War Memorial, 1962

Goodison, James, Franks, Norman, *Over Paid, Over Sexed and Over Here*, Wingham Press, 1991

Griffin, John, Kostenuk, Samuel, *RCAF Squadron Histories and Aircraft, 1924–1968*, Samuel Stevens Hakkert, 1977

Gunby, David, Temple, Pelham, *Bomber Losses in the Middle East and Mediterranean Vols 1 and 2*, Midland Publishing/Air Britain, 2006–2018

Hallam, Sqn Ldr T. D., *The Spider Web: The Romance of a Flying Boat Flight in the First World War*, William Blackwood, 1919

Halley, James, *The Squadrons of the Royal Air Force & Commonwealth 1918–1988*, Air Britain 1988

Haugland, Vern, *The Eagle Squadrons: Yanks in the RAF, 1940-1942*, David and Charles, 1979

Henshaw, Trevor, *The Sky their Battlefield II: Air Fighting and Air Casualties of the Great War. British, Commonwealth and United States Air Services 1912 to 1919*, Fetubi, 2014

Herington, John, *Australians in the War 1939-45, Series 3 Vol. 3*, Halstead Press, 1962

Herington, John, *Air War against Germany and Italy*, Australian War Memorial, 1954

Hobson, Chris with Noble, Andrew, *Falklands Air War*, Midland, 2002

Horn, Alex, *Wings over the Pacific: The RNZAF in the Pacific War*, Random, 1992

Horsfall, Jack, Cave, Nigel, *Mons 1914*, Pen & Sword, 2000

Hunt, Leslie, *Twenty-One Squadrons: History of the Royal Auxiliary Air Force, 1925-1957*, Garnstone Press, 1972

Jefford, Wg Cdr C. G., *RAF Squadrons: A Comprehensive Record of the Movement and Equipment of All RAF Squadrons and Their Antecedents Since 1912*, Airlife, 1988/2001

Kumar, Air Mshl Bharat, *An Incredible War: IAF in Kashmir War 1947-1948*, Centre for Air Power Studies, 2007

Louw, Martin, Bouwer, Stefaan, *The South African Air Force at War: A Pictorial Appraisal* (Second Edition), C. van Rensburg Publications, 1995

Low, Ron, *83 Squadron 1917-1969*, Private, 1992

McLean, Steven, *Squadrons of the SAAF and their Aircraft 1920-2005*, Interpak Books, 2005

McNeill, Ross, *Royal Air Force Coastal Command Losses: Vol 1. Aircraft and Crew Losses, 1939–1941*, Midland, 2003

Mason, Francis K., *Hawks Rising: The Story of 25 Squadron Royal Air Force*, Air Britain, 2001

Middlebrook, Martin, *The Nuremberg Raid*, Allen Lane, 1973

Middlebrook, Martin, Everitt, Chris, *The Bomber Command War Diaries*, Midland, 2011

Milberry, Larry, Halliday, Hugh, *The Royal Canadian Air Force at War 1939-1945*, Canav Books, 1990

Mitchell, Alan W., *New Zealanders in the Air War*, Harrap, 1945

Morse, Stan (Ed.), *Gulf Air War: Debrief*, Aerospace, 1991

Moyes, Philip, *Bomber Squadrons of the RAF and their Aircraft*. Macdonald & Co., 1964

Napier, Michael, *RAF Tornado Units in Combat 1992–2019*, Osprey, 2021

Niestlé, Axel, *German U-boat Losses During World War II*, Frontline, 2014

Official, *The RCAF Overseas – The First Four Years*, Oxford University Press, Toronto, 1944

Official, *The Royal Indian Air Force at War: An Account of Air Operations Against the Japanese in South-East Asia*, Director of Public Relations, GHQ Delhi, 1946

Parry, Simon, *Battle of Britain Combat Archive Vols. 1–12*, Red Kite, 2015 *et seq.*

Parry, Simon, *Dunkirk: Air Combat Archive, 21 May–2 June 1940*, Red Kite, 2017

Paul, Air Cdre Christopher, *Sing High: History of 90 Squadron, Royal Flying Corps and Royal Air Force, 1917–1965*, 90 Squadron Association, 1989

Price, Alfred, *Aircraft versus Submarine*, William Kimber, 1973/1980

Price, Alfred, *Instruments of Darkness: The History of Electronic Warfare, 1939–1945*, Macdonald and Jane's, 1977

Raleigh, Sir Walter and Jones, H. A., *The War in the Air Vols. I–VII*, OUP, 1922–37

Rawlings, John D. R., *Fighter Squadrons of the RAF and their Aircraft*, Macdonald, 1969

Rawlings, John D. R., *Coastal Support and Special Squadrons of the RAF and their aircraft*, Jane's, 1982

Revel, Alex, *Baptism of Fire: The Royal Flying Corps At War: The First Year In France 1914-1915*, Wickford Books, 2018

Richards, Denis, Saunders, Hilary S., *RAF 1939–1945*, HMSO, 1954

Ritchie, Dr Sebastian, *The RAF Small Wars and Insurgencies in the Middle East, 1919–1939*, Air Historical Branch, 2011

Ritchie, Dr Sebastian, *The RAF Small Wars and Insurgencies: Later Colonial Operations 1945–1975*, Air Historical Branch 2011

Rogan, Eugene, *The Fall of the Ottomans: The Great War in the Middle East 1914–1920*, Penguin, 2015

Ross, Sqn Ldr J. M. S., *Royal New Zealand Air Force: Official History*, Official, 1955

Rudge, Chris, *Air-to-Air: The Story Behind the Air Combat Claims of the RNZAF*, Adventure Air, 2003

Sabharwal, Wg Cdr D. P., *COBRAS: 3 Squadron, Indian Air Force Diamond Jubilee*, Private, 2002

Schoemann, Michael, *Springbok Fighter Victory: SAAF Fighter Operations Vols. 1–6*, Freeworld, 2002–2012

Shores, Christopher et al, *Above the Trenches*, Grub Street, 1990

Shores, Christopher, Williams, Clive, *Aces High Vol. 1*, Grub Street, 1994

Shores, Christopher, Williams, Clive, *Aces High Vol. 2*, Grub Street, 1999

Shores, Christopher, *Air War for Burma*, Grub Street 2005

Shores, Christopher, Cull, Brian with Malizia, Nicola, *Air War for Yugoslavia, Greece and Crete*, Grub Street, 1987

Shores, Christopher, Cull, Brian, *Bloody Shambles Vol. 1*, Grub Street 1991

Shores, Christopher, Cull, Brian, *Bloody Shambles Vol. 2*, Grub Street 1993

Shores, Christopher, *Dust Clouds over the Middle East*, Grub Street, 1996

Shores, Christopher, *Fledgling Eagles*, Grub Street, 1991

Shores, Christopher et al., *A History of the Mediterranean Air War Vols. 1–5*, Grub Street, 2012–2021

Shores, Christopher, Cull, Brian with Malizia, Nicola, *Malta: The Hurricane Years 1940-41*, Grub Street, 1987

Shores, Christopher and Cull, Brian with Malizia, Nicola, *Malta: The Spitfire Year 1942*, Grub Street, 1988

Shores, Christopher, *Those Other Eagles*, Grub Street, 2004

Singh, Pushpindar, *The Battle Axes: No. 7 Squadron Indian Air Force 1942–1992*, Society of Aerospace Studies, New Delhi, 1993

Smith, John T., *Gone to Russia to Fight: RAF in South Russia 1918–1920*, Amberley, 2010

Sturtivant, Ray and Balance, Theo, *The Squadrons of the Fleet Air Arm*, Air Britain, 1994

Strachan, Hew, *The First World War in Africa*, Oxford University Press, 2004

Thomas, Chris, Shores, Christopher, *2nd Tactical Air Force Vols. 1-4*, Classic Publications, 2005–2008

Wynn, Kenneth G., *Men of the Battle of Britain: A Biographical Directory of the Few*, Frontline, 2015

# INDEX